DOVE

DOVE is a collection of essays, stories, observations, prayers, and poetry. It is a personal witness to history by one on a spiritual quest. It is a voyage through the 20th Century seen through the eyes of a newspaper woman, mother, wife, and spiritual seeker who has heard the small, still Voice. If, as it is said, that an unexamined life is without value, then Margaret Taylor Gilmore's life is pure gold.

- Lawrence Wertan, Publisher

*Especially
for
Michelle
With Love*

Margaret Taylor Gilmore

DOVE

Margaret Taylor Gilmore

A Boxer Publishing Book

Boxer Publishing, LLC
P. O. Box 971
Toccoa, Georgia 30577
United States
Tel: 706-886-9571
www.boxerpublishing.com
boxerbooks@alltel.net
Cover Art: Alice Ward
Interior Illustrations: Alice Ward
Technical Assistance: Cyndi Sherrard
First Edition: Spring 2006
ISBN: 0-9653624-4-2
Cataloging in Publication (CIP)
Printed in the United States of America
Library of Congress Control Number: 2006923681

Table of Contents

Interpretation

It has been said the heart is a lonely hunter. My heart is in this book.

Throughout the years I have hunted for words to write, thinking I could describe my heart in them. In this book are words that may awaken memories of someone's longing to express emotions too deep to describe. The lonely hunter remembers the times, the places, the people and the sometimes sacred and secret moments that overwhelmed the heart...with inexpressible knowing.

Margaret Taylor Gilmore
Written March 18, 2005

Acknowledgements

I can write, but I am at a loss for words to express the depth and sincerity of my gratitude for the ways these people have helped me bring birth to this book.

Emily Watson's faith is stubborn. She never doubted I would one day publish a book of my writings. When two of my long-time friends heard me say it would be impossible to sort through literally thousands of files, folders and scraps of papers, to create a book, I began to believe it could happen.

Betty Settle, experienced in legal matters, said she would "love to help", and did so, by cheerfully encouraging me, and by giving several months of her Monday mornings, helping to separate hundreds of articles into categories, filing them by subjects and titles.

Then came Alice Ward, multitalented, a recognized painter of glorious oils and incredibly fast at whatever she does, is also skilled in the technology of printing. She gave generously of her time and talents. She has translated all those typewritten pages into the technical language required by a publisher of books.

"Dove", the book's cover, was painted by Alice Ward. For this, and for her generosity, I have only this to say, "My cup runneth over with thankful love."

Margaret Taylor Gilmore
January 2006

About the Artist

Alice Ward is legally blind. She has a genetically limited imperfection that also inhibits the sight of both her children. In spite of this, each of them uses their inherited talent to create canvas and poetry that reflect their appreciation for the gift of life. Alice is the inspiration for this book.

Alice's paintings are currently displayed in homes and offices across several continents. Her love and her laughter, her skill at the computer and her stubborn insistence that I not grow weary and give up on *"Dove"* is a gift I now share with you who read and revel in the examples of Alice's beautiful art.

"Beginnings" by Alice Ward

Life Story

An Almost Perfect Dove

Carved from what appeared to me to be alabaster stone, it was cool to my touch, and had the look of softness. It was a white dove, and it felt like poetry in my cupped hands.

I wondered about it, because it was perfect in every way, except for a brown spot about the size of a quarter near the base of one wing.

The price on the sticker was not formidable, but was a bit more than I would have guessed it would be, given the spot that spoiled the perfection a purchaser probably would desire. The mystery eluded me as to why someone had chosen to use an imperfect stone to carve such a perfect symbol of perfect peace.

I held the dove, and in my hand it felt as if it belonged there. Belonged ...somewhere in my heart. I paid for it, took it home and for several months considered it a rare treasure that I would keep for always.

Then December came and my mind turned to gifts and giving. That was when I thought of a dear friend who has a generous spirit, a keen mind and a remarkable talent she shares liberally. She paints in oils the beautiful things she sees.

But...Alice has a rare genetically inherited flaw that renders her to be legally blind. With limited vision in one eye and without education in art, she paints canvases that are exquisite and detailed, colorful expressions of sensitivity to her surroundings.

Alice is generous. She sometimes gives paintings to help support schools and churches. She gives generously to friends because she is truly grateful to God for enabling her to live, love, paint and often to laugh, because she knows nobody's perfect.

And that is why I knew I had to give Alice the dove. Because the thought came to me that it may have been the one who carved the almost perfect dove, decided to let the dark spot remain, because it represented confession of a longing, knowing all the while that perfection is not possible for a human person, but longing for perfection is an instinctive part of being a spiritual being.

Margaret Taylor Gilmore
September 26, 2002

A Dove Descending

In our garden there is a little tree they tell us ought not to be there. It isn't native to this state, nor to this country. But it has lived here for many years, alone and distinctly different from the giant oaks, dogwoods and pines that stand around it.

Each year I think it has finally died, but in late spring the spindly little tree, with its spindly little limbs, sprouts out large leafs that look far too large for the size of the branches. In autumn they do not quickly dry up and blow away. Instead, as they finally fall, they cover the earth nearby with a carpet of gold that survives long after other growths have been raked away.

And once again this spring, the little tree became mother to one single bud that became a firm, hard and heavy, perfectly round ball that hangs tenaciously at the very tip end of one of the fragile looking branches. I have learned these nuts are rich in a kind of oil that is valuable in several ways to industry. Perhaps the tree isn't lonely, because she knows who knows and cares what happens within her every year.

I feel a kinship with this tree. Each time I walk nearby I touch a leaf and speak thankfully to the life that is evident in it. I too have been a single mother with one child. I too have sometimes felt alone among all the others. Sometimes I think about trees, creatures and people who sometimes feel most alone when they find themselves one among many.

I remember a verse in the Bible that mentions a lonely sparrow on a rooftop and I think about eagles that fly alone, and doves that have voices that makes one think of loneliness. Then I am reminded the words solitude and silence do not always mean sadness. Deliberately giving ones self a time to spend in silent solitude can bring the beginning of mental/spiritual healing. Because in an hour spent alone and in absolute stillness, one can often hear, like a dove descending, the gentle, soft voice of belonging...and feel a peace coming to rest somewhere deep within...

I need to ask someone...if I could save the tree's child when it appears to be ready to fall, and if I buried it in a pot of soil and left it alone awhile, might it sprout and grow? If I could save the life that lies within that nut, I would believe even more in miracles. But I need no other proof. Miracles have been happening around me all my life. If God knows when a sparrow is born, and when it dies, is it not possible He will be watching over one seed, full of life, buried in a clay pot, waiting for His touch to become a miracle? Ought I ask for more?

Margaret Taylor Gilmore
September 14, 2005

Images

Images...memories of things seen, strong impressions, voices and certain portions of isolated moments sometimes surface at unexpected moments and I always wonder why. However, I do believe there is meaning and a purpose for everything that happens to us.

I do not understand what brings such specific images to my mind at the times they come, but when they come, I am always strangely reassured that beyond time and distance and even beyond death, I am remembered and loved.

And I am inclined to believe especially in the significance of those sudden flashes of memory that come so vividly, like those split second sightings of a familiar highway sign we catch a glimpse of in the dark as we race along, hoping we are still on the right road.

Because in most cases, in those "sudden sightings" that at first seem totally unrelated to whatever is the prevailing "winds" that are blowing in my life at the moment, I have been amazed to find direction, reassurance and release of tensions in my body.

In a paper, written during a "low period" in my life I wrote: Perhaps, today if I write these thoughts into visible images the ache in my heart will go away.

I see that "lonely sparrow on the rooftop" mentioned in the Bible, and I feel a real kinship with the small bird I once saw pictured in a painting. The bird is waiting out the storm, its head under its wing, its feet clinging to a small wire, while all around, fierce winds blow and rain falls in torrents.

And I remember hearing someone tell a story about a little boy walking with his father across a rough, newly plowed field. The child tries to keep up, and clings tightly to his father's hand. Finally, his little legs growing weary, he says, "Daddy, I'm too tired to keep on holding to your hand. Now I need you to hold onto mine."

Today I am the sparrow, the bird in the storm, and I am much in need of permission to let go of trying to be strong and brave. I truly long for a solid shoulder to lean on and feel the safety of being in the comforting, reassuring arms of the Everlasting.

Hear my prayer, O Lord, hear my prayer. I need to feel loved. Forgive me, please Jesus, for complaining. Please accept my prayer of thanksgiving for your love that has kept me safe thus far. Thank you for loving memories that bless and burn, and for the way you always manage to speak to me in the storm, always with the same words..."Trust Me."

Now as I contemplate, allowing my mind to wander through recent memories, the image that comes to me is that of yesterday and suddenly seeing in a cloudless blue sky, a flock of white birds, winging in perfect, graceful formation toward a destination...to a distant place God has already given them instinct to find. I know that soon they will arrive safely there, where their hearts and their wings will have rest from the stresses of time, distance and storms that they have met along their way.

Thank you, O Heavenly Father, for giving me images of love and reassurance and for your voice, promising to guide me instinctively, daily, every moment of all my life, all the way home.

Margaret Taylor Gilmore
December 16, 2001

A Challenge to be Met

If, one day I would dare to share
with the whole world,
emotions and the evolving events
that have colored the canvas
of my life, would I be wise,
or foolish?

If one who writes about
what really matters, mattered,
and still matters
and when seeing it revealed,
if the whole world would tear
apart the telling,
would that not really matter?

What I have written,
I have written.
No matter what happens
next to me, those
moments I have written...mattered.
Really mattered.

There are lines I have written
to preserve forever...memories of moments
that shimmered in my heart, and each time
when I remember them...my emotions moved
as if to the music of my mother's crystal wind
chimes...moving softly in a breeze,
sparkling in the window of a sun filled room.

I made records of that memory
because it mattered,
really mattered, and I felt
the beauty of it in my deepest soul.

Other times I have written
to chart the courses I have taken
to find solace, and have learned
that some grief can only be

assuaged by accepting the pain,
because there is always a Gethsemane
to bear sometime along the way
to higher grounds.

But as yet for now, I am still unwilling
to go out naked before the world...
naked on white pages,
my deepest self revealed on lines of type
that are the soul prints
of my life history story,
and contain self portraits of
the realest parts of me.

Is who I am and what I am
a fragile, delicate, uncertain
soul who only imagines
that what I write might somehow
be good enough to share
with others somewhere?

Or will I forever hide
behind the lines
of paragraphs I write?
Or will I someday dare
to confess I've cared
and cried, because I've tried,
and failed, and loved and lost,
and sometimes questioned God?

And in desperation, or
in ecstasy I have translated
those experienced essences
of my life into words
on pages of white paper.

Is my reluctance to "go public"
because I have forgotten how God
has enabled me, through many storms,
to be brave, strong and resilient,
supplied with courage and faith?
I wonder why I now am insecure,
and afraid to dare to share and say so?

Or does it mean I am vain,
fearful of being known,
unmasked, revealed and recognized
perhaps, as being not the one
I have seemed to be?

Or does it mean, perhaps,
the one with who I struggle
to find answers, has more
for me to learn about myself?

Now I believe before
I can feel free
to release the manuscripts
that tell of all those marvelous, mysterious,
life moments...

Reading this I have come to believe
I must wait to hear from on high.

So...if, or when the time may come for me
to dare to go naked before the world,
God will show me how and when and where.
Meanwhile, as long as I keep on loving,
I will keep on writing words my heart dictates,
because I am content if God is the only one
who reads what I have written.

Margaret Taylor Gilmore
May 19, 1995

Somewhere

She is out there, somewhere...
I will find her, I will find her...Someday...
Perhaps, on a golden afternoon in springtime,
as I walk along some country path, from the distance
I will see her beckoning me to come to her...
or from within a quiet forest where tall trees made
wonderful cathedrals, carpeted in soft green moss and little grasses...perhaps, I
will hear her call to me, and I will
find her waiting for me. I will find her, she will be
somewhere.

Perhaps, at some unexpected moment, someone will reach to
take my hand, and someone will welcome me, and lead me to a
new-old space in time. And perhaps that someone will be
she...

I lost her somewhere, sometime.
And lately I have missed her...dreadfully...
Now I wistfully seek to find her...
And I am sure that she is somewhere.
And lately, now and then, along my way,
I've thought I glimpsed her,
fleetingly...
in lovely mountain places,
in music too beautiful to bear,
and when I kneel to pray...

Yesterday...
I thought I heard a voice,
thought I glimpsed a face,
among my memory's chest of colleted treasures.
I think I've found her. The girl I lost for a while,
the girl I used to be.
She'd been tucked into the pages
of the book of the chapters of my life...
and she was waiting there for me.
Waiting to be remembered...

She was never lost. It was I.
I am the part of us that hurried on ahead one day,
to find my way through our journey of life.
I am the one, not she, who has been lost awhile,
among the busy, noisy years.
I think I have found her.
The girl that I was...I am.
My body bears the weight of time,
but the girl I thought was lost
is the part of me that is
a spirit that years cannot erase.
I am younger...now that we are found.

Margaret Taylor Gilmore
1993

Concept of Time

I will go back awhile, into time to find myself, perhaps. My world was larger then, quieter, safer, and greener, too.

Daddies were taller, trees were shadier, trips were longer, and Saturdays were a long way apart.

I remember bed slats, crazy quilts, featherbeds and windows in my room, propped open with sawed off broom handles.

At my house we had button boxes and screen doors, and front porches with rocking chairs.

In the woods, springs were sparklier and deeper, little flowers were sweeter smelling.

Baby chickens were yellowier and softer, and tight little flower buds took an awfully long time to unfold and turn into roses.

I remember wood boxes behind the kitchen stove, and ovens that kept bread warm until suppertime. I remember dippers with long handles, and cold drinks of water that spilled down my chin.

Grandparents were older, school was scarier, clocks struck louder at night, and Christmases were years away.

Peaches were juicier, rounder, fuzzier, apples were redder and too big to hold with one hand. Autumn leaves were cracklier, snow was deeper, ice cream was special and Sundays were grand!

I remember wall calendars with beautiful pictures that we kept even after December to remind us of all the wonderful things we had seen and done in the long, beautiful months of the year that had lasted so well.

My world is smaller now. Solitude is harder to find. I am smaller, too, than I had thought. I think, because I'm seeing eternity...and time must be larger than I had believed.

Now I know that life is neither short nor long...it is both!

I am pondering my past, and I find I am richer than I realized, having had a childhood in a REALLY BIG world, where everything was bigger and lasted a long, long time. Now I think I see that time was...and I am. Grandpa was and daddy was. I am. We were, and time is....US!

Life's a very BIG experience I am glad I didn't miss, along my way in time.

Margaret Taylor Gilmore

Identifying God

I have written about God, and how I have found our connecting points especially at times of prayer and worship. I have written meditatively about my private, early wakening hours at home and while worshiping Sunday mornings in St. Michael's.

Who is Jesus, who is God, who is The Holy Spirit? How shall I trust Him, how shall I worship Him? By what name shall I call Him when I pray?

Now I write to describe how I grew from a childhood simplicity of believing, to spiritual maturity that has brought me full circle from childhood's trusting what I was taught by other's example, to an incalculable scope of personal "seeing" for myself who He is...I am now back to the simplicity of certainty that Jesus loves me...This I know, by way of my life-long learning experiences that have taught me to speak of Him as The Presence of my God.

Today I began to try to trace the beginnings of when that Presence began to become a personal relationship.

The little lady who was my first Sunday School teacher taught me to sing, "Jesus loves me this I know, for the Bible tells me so." And she gave me little cards with pictures of a tall man holding a baby lamb. I looked at the pictures of Jesus and did not question who my teacher said He was. And I did not doubt He was someone very important. If Mrs. Stilwell said it was so, then I knew it had to be true. So I sang that I knew He loved me as He loved the little lambs, because she had taught me to believe what the song said.

Besides that, I knew for sure there was a someone somewhere whose name was God, because I heard my grandparents talk about Him, and I did not question that He was the one about whom there were many stories in our big Bible.

Most of all, each evening before bedtime, I heard my grandparents talk about ME when they prayed. This made me feel a bit uncomfortable because this God was obviously a very important person and I wasn't sure He really knew about me. I hadn't quite gotten the connection between Mrs. Stilwell's Jesus and my grandparent's big God. But what I felt then I know now was the beginning of my emotions of instinctive awe, reverence and worship just hearing the names of Jesus and God.

It was when I had grown to adulthood, and had learned to pray to whomever it was who seemed always to be ever present in my deepest self, that I gradually knew was the Jesus God whom I had met when I was a very young child. The Presence who had always been there, tugging at my heart when my emotions surged with compassion, appreciation, amazement, gratitude, love and longing. This, I knew, held the keys to my life's moments, glad, sad, and I sensed that all my life's pathway was known to Him.

The most profound experience that confirmed my mature relationship with The Lord God Almighty came on a sunny Sunday morning when I knelt at the altar and for the first time to participate in taking communion at St. Michael's Episcopal Church in Charleston. Since that day, the wafer and the cup have become all sufficient for my every need.

For as I take the bread of life, my physical body is nourished, and as the wine touches my lips I am healed of all my hurts and forgiven for all my foolish ways. Then I rise from the altar to kneel again in thanksgiving when I have returned to my place among others in the sanctuary.

Awe and wonder, wonder and reverence, reverence and an ineffable sense of the presence of the God of God, Very God of Very God gives joyful peace to my soul.

Margaret Taylor Gilmore
July 16, 2001

Does God have White Hair?

Sometimes when someone has asked me, "How would you describe God?" or "How would He look physically and His day-to-day personally?", the more I thought about it, the more I knew the answer...I think he'd look like Grandpa Taylor. Hugh Johnson Taylor was my paternal grandfather. Today, contemplating how much like him, I know that I am, could also partly describe my relationship to God. I bear in my physical body the likeness of Grandpa, and the Bible tells me I am created in the image of God. I am kin to both of them, Grandpa and God seem somehow to define the word "love" to me.

I was always a bit afraid of Grandpa, even though he never once raised his hand or his voice to punish me. Sometimes I could hear his gravelly "Humph" from the back of his throat when I was about to do something inappropriate. His reproaches were gentle, too. I've been told people remember the day when he saw me biting into a green apple and he said, "I hate to see you eating that apple." And they told me, I turned my back to him and said, "Now you can't see me."

I knew he was happy when Grandma told him I had done or said in school that pleased her, and she knew Grandpa would be pleased, too. He didn't tell me, but Grandma said he was pleased when he learned I had done or said something that made something better or clearer.

If I ever thought about the word love and wondered, I know I always felt safe with Grandpa. A lifetime later, I realize it was complete confidence in the love of God that made him feel secure in being the man he was.

I am part of God and part of Grandfather...We are linked by earthly and heavenly love. I recognize I have inherited Fatherly love, when at some moment something causes me to pause and rethink some act or word. I believe such moments are God's way to remind me He is faithful to keep His promises to keep forever whatever I have promised to keep for Him.

I remember how Grandpa looked...he had bushy white eyebrows and white hair and wherever I was...eating, sleeping, doing, being...God and Grandpa were never far away, and that description seems right to me.

Margaret T. Gilmore

As Good as His Word

Grandpa Taylor believed a man was good as his word. The story of his life is set in a time in America's history that is almost forgotten today. The account of how he came to own the property, the house and the acres where I grew up, will sound like fiction. But, I was there when Grandpa's faith in his fellowman was lived out before my eyes.

Grandpa was born in Tennessee. He married Margaret Robbins and they had two daughters and two sons, but Margaret died young and Grandpa married Alice Norman, who accepted the children, and they loved her.

During an especially rainy season, the boys suffered colds and earaches. Grandpa was advised they needed to live in a drier climate, so he loaded the family and their belongings on a covered wagon and they traveled across the country to Medford, Oregon. There Grandpa purchased an apple orchard. However, a few years later a disease struck the trees and the orchard died.

Grandpa was not defeated. It gave him opportunity to see more of the country. He took his family to Arkansas and brought a farm where they lived comfortably for several years. By this time, one daughter had died, the other had married, and both sons had spent several months in the Army serving in France during World War I.

Grandpa was getting restless...When he saw a notice in the *"Cappers Weekly"* that a fellow in the Arkansas Valley of Colorado wanted to exchange farms and equipment, house, livestock, and all, with someone in Arkansas, willing to trade farm for farm, house and equipment, the idea appealed to Grandpa. He wrote to describe his farm and equipment. After several letters, they agreed that on a certain day of the month each owner would depart the farm and leave the deed of ownership in the local bank where it would remain until the new owner appeared and identified himself, then the deal would be completed.

I clearly remember the day, driving along the road to the front of the house, Grandpa said, "This is it." Then he asked Grandma, "Shall we go in now, or should we go to the bank first and get the deed?"

"Go to the bank first", she replied...and we did. It was a little bank in a little town. I was five years old and I do not recall any problem at any point during the entire process...If there had been, I believe I would have known.

Later, Grandpa said he'd had word the deal was satisfactory on both sides. We never saw the man whose name I knew only as Mr. Griffin, and they never corresponded again. I grew up in that new place and both grandparents died there.

I spent a quiet, mostly private childhood and I am often reminded how privileged I was to grow up in such a time as this story is set.

However, I do dimly recall that those were harsh years economically and the nation was suffering, but the War to End Wars had been won, and gradually America became wealthy and proud and began to doubt any man's word or handshake could be as binding as a lawyer's legal document.

This is a true story.

Margaret Taylor Gilmore

Icons of the Twentieth Century

"A powerful and provocative look at the giants of the last one hundred years – the groundbreakers, thought provokers, visionaries, tyrants, trendsetter and style makers who have left an indelible mark on our time..."

I found this description in a catalog listing of "Best Books." The words set me to wondering. Who's an icon? Have I ever met an icon? Who would I name first if I were to be asked?

I suppose most people, if asked, could name a person whose example, words or personal presence in their lives stands out in their minds as being the person, the one event, or the one moment that has influenced them most fundamentally.

At the top of my own personal Icon list there is my paternal grandfather, Hugh Johnson Taylor. He is the one, whom since childhood, I have always considered as always being "at the head of our house." His influence shaped my life's philosophy. He articulated little in regard to what he believed to be the way to live, day by day, but my life today reflects what I learned from living the first nineteen years of my life in the home he provided for my father and me when my mother died. Even today, many years since, I frequently recognize in my words and my strong spiritual convictions that I am very much like him and the example he set for me as I was growing up. I was and am still proud to be like him.

There were other people whose influence guided me in choices that resulted in helping me discover my talents. And there were individuals who encouraged me to attempt tasks for which I had no experience but presented opportunities that ultimately revealed strengths and intellectual ability of which I had been unaware. And I saw at first hand other examples of lives being lived according to solid spiritual anchors of faith in The Almighty.

And especially...throughout my growing up years I was being subtly influenced by my grandmother. Quietly she moved through her days, seeming never to complain or to question her life pathway. Being the second wife of the husband whom she always referred as "Mr. Taylor," and being mother to a little girl to whom she was all that any child could ask or need. I do not recall ever hearing her raise her voice. But I do remember hearing her singing sometimes. And the song I remember hearing was "Bringing in the Sheaves." That melody still rings in my memory, and I remember especially some of the lines, one of which goes, "When the reaping is over we shall come rejoicing, bringing in the sheaves." It must have been her favorite for it is the one she sang most often.

I especially recall that every afternoon on my way home from school as soon as I came through the gate I would start calling her name. And I remember now, with warmth and a reverence that still catches at my throat that Grandma was always there when I called her. Also that she was always forgiving, indulgent and most of all, she was gentle in every way. I think it was her quietness, her delicacy of form and manner, her fair skin, blue eyes and her golden hair that became faded to a soft undertone that retained a hint of its glory that I now remember most clearly about her.

I remember thinking she and Grandpa looked "nice" on the Sunday mornings when they started out to go to church. Grandpa with his big black hat and suit, and Grandma in her Sunday dress with ruffles at the neck.

I am thankful for my Taylor grandparents and I would list them as MY Icons. For they gave me examples of the way that if lived, I would find light for my life pathway and assurance it would last until evening time when all of us will come home, joyfully bringing in the sheaves that represent the work we have done for The Master in the fields where we have labored.

Margaret Taylor Gilmore
November 22, 2002

Remembrance of Things That Have Mattered

Thoughts Before Sunrise
(Lines from my Journal)

I've watched and worked and played and prayed
throughout these many years.
I've wondered, and wandered and struggled and sighed,
trying to fit into a "perfect place."
I've read and I've reasoned,
I've listened...and impulsively, sometimes,
I've followed my heart.

Throughout the years,
most all of the time, every day, every hour,
I've wanted to know answers...
Answers to questions,
most of which I could never
quite fully define.

Who am I? Why am I? Why?
And does it, do I...really matter?
I still ask the sort of questions today
that I have always asked,
and still I wait for perfect answers.

One thing I have discovered...
When, now and then, I have
given up asking for EXACT answers,
then my mind becomes easier.
I've learned if I follow
my deepest instincts,
without explanation why,
my heart leads my feet
and I am seldom wrong.

And in my most holy moments
in perfect solitude, all questions dissolve.
Wrapped in the arms of my "other self",
lost is my need to ask why or who,
certain only of the Presence of God.

Then I sense that this is where I began,
and this is where the end of me will be.

Lord, help me to always remember,
there are no perfect questions here,
and the perfect answers are holy mysteries.

And that is answer enough for me.
Almost.

Margaret T. Gilmore

Who Am I, Lord?

Who am I Lord? Who am I...now that I have accumulated more years than I had expected to count...or ever wanted to count?

Who am I Lord? I am a name, I have a number in the phone book, I am listed in a church directory of members. I have a face I see in my mirror. But lately, Lord, I sense I am losing the who that I am. As I walk through the streets and into the shops, the way I see myself in other people's eyes is changing from what for most of my life I have been accustomed to seeing. Most people are vaguely uncomfortable in the presence of "older people."

And who is this individual who is in some reluctant state between the me I know that I am, with the me that is growing more and more insistent that I am not the me I have always thought to be.

What do I fear about growing older? Is it a fear of losing my identity? As I move about among the people on the street, sometimes I feel I am invisible. Other times I am treated with such tender caution I fear they fear I may suddenly shatter into small pieces. I am not comfortable being old...

Now I am remembering how little I was aware of how my grandparents were feeling about themselves as aging people. Now I often wish with all my heart I had known then what I realize now about how young they were in the days when I was growing up in their home. Perhaps some time we will talk together about that. I have lots of questions now to ask about their lives before I was born.

Now I am learning to depend upon the all sufficient mercies of the Almighty God to lead me gently into my real future.

Margaret Taylor Gilmore

To be a Witness

I have a habit of jotting down on any paper I can find bits and pieces of fascinating thoughts and intriguing quotes I find in unexpected places. With not enough time to read or copy more of the quote, I sometimes forget about the paper until I find it, sometimes long after when I'm home again and the jacket or purse I used that day hasn't been out of the closet for a long time.

Such was the discovery on January 31, 2003, of a tightly folded piece, torn from the top of a newspaper. The dateline reads: *San Francisco 1988*. I remember the place and the year, and have tried to remember exactly where I encountered the thought. I do remember the words made me stop and jot them down because I needed to think more about that concept...it read:

> *"To be a witness does not consist in engaging in propaganda or even in stirring people up, but it means in being a living mystery. It means to live in such a way that our life would not make sense if God did not exist."*
> *(Quote by Cardinal Segfred, Archbishop of Paris)*

On the opposite corner I had copied another quote. This one has no credit line. I have wondered if this might also be by the Archbishop. Perhaps he wrote these mysterious words when he was experiencing a dark night of his soul:

> *"...Adrift, but with faith, direction, scrutiny...,still very lonely, self confrontational, evaluative..."*

The Bishop's contemplative self-examination makes me think his thoughts are not unlike those a great many of us might have written. We wonder, we pray, and by example we can become a witness to others that draws them to us because we are obviously following a mysterious and powerful guide.

And now and then when for a while, we have a period when we feel adrift and lonely, but by believing, trusting in God, even in the dark, we find our way through the wilderness. Life is a mystery. We are all mysteries, because we are not just a body with a spirit, we are a spirit that has a body. And only the Holy Spirit knows exactly who we are.

Margaret Taylor Gilmore
February 1, 2003

A Week of Wonder

Monday

There was a meeting of Mocking Birds, gathered together in trees where I live. First I heard one singing from somewhere at the back of my house. "Interesting," I thought, "He must have chosen a new stage. Until today he has always sung from a tree near the front of the house."

I opened my front door to stand on the porch to welcome the day with a prayer of thanksgiving. Just at that moment a burst of music came from directly overhead. It was not just one Mocking Bird, it was several Mocking Birds, taking turns, sometimes singing together, sometimes solo.

They sang non-stop for several minutes. I was awed, because it was as if I was present to hear a grand composition, written by a master composer. It was a symphony. To me it was music of the spheres, performed by earth-born winged things.

Wednesday

We had driven many miles through forests, then across flat, sandy acres to a remote place, finally arriving at the edge of a large river. There was a long pier and a dock, but no boats nor people other than the friend who had brought me there.

I walked alone to stand at the edge of the pier to meet the moment I sensed was about to come. I believe the Almighty God prepares a time and a place for us, now and then, from which we may gain a glimpse of heaven.

The sky was the kind poets write about and painters try to capture on canvas. A few clouds, like fragile white feathers, floated across the soft blueness of the sky. The waters were calm, the wind was soft.

Then a wide-winged bird appeared, seeming for a moment to be exactly over my head. Not near, but close enough to cause me to feel the bird saw me, and knew that I saw him. Onward and upward he flew, and I watched until he disappeared into the blue mists of the distances far beyond where I could follow. It was a holy moment, and as I returned to my friend, I knew I had seen earth and sky meet at the horizon, and I had been nearer to heaven than I had ever been before...Because I had seen it through the eyes of a white bird.

Saturday

Azaleas were at their height of glory, and trailing wisteria dressed in lavender and miniature climbing yellow roses had bloomed to be a part of the astonishing revelation of April in South Carolina's Lowcountry.

My daily walk includes a tour of the gardens where I live, then I take time to pause at the foot of a tremendous old tree that is covered with Spanish moss. Its bark is white and its branches are completely bare, except for the thick overlay of moss which long ago began to smother it with long fronds of gray. I've loved that old dead tree. I have always admired and appreciated it because throughout the year it presents such a distinctively dramatic addition to the landscape of where I live...

No one knows how old it is, but everyone believes it has been dead for more years than people living in the big house up front can remember. Visitors always comment on the ghostly drama of that tree and someone always advises us, "That tree is dead. It should be cut down. It could be dangerous."

This morning, already nostalgic, regretting how quickly the azalea blossoms have begun to fade, I walked across the pathway to marvel again at the sight of "my old dead tree." What I saw was so astonishing it took some moments before I could believe what had happened, seemingly overnight.

I felt as if I was experiencing something like what happened to those men on the road to Emmaus. I wondered if my eyes were deceiving me. Great clusters of green, green leaves were emerging as if escaping from the moss. Not from just a few branches here and there, but all over the tree, stubby branches were bursting with new life.

"He's ALIVE!", I said aloud, "He's alive!" And then I knew I had experienced another holy moment. I knew I had witnessed a miracle, and I couldn't wait to tell someone. The next morning after church, I told friends, "You have got to come see that tree."

I do not know why all this has happened to me this week, but I do not need to wonder. I need only to try to express to the Almighty how thankful I am that He has arranged my life to see earth meet heaven, hear music of the spheres and then to witness a ressurection..all three in one week. Now I think blessed is a more accurate word to spell what I am.

Margaret Taylor Gilmore
April 13, 2005

Phoenix

I meditate
and wait to find illusive
answers that have escaped me
in my busy, frantic, searching hours.

I ask myself
and I question others,
and I find no perfect answers,
nor perfect people,
nor perfect questions, even.

But sometimes I find
larger questions.
My thoughts search up and down
the crowded stairways of my days,
and at night through the dark,
subterranean tunnels
of my memories.

My soul asks probing, insistent questions
of my heart, and sometimes
the probing over turn
secret, hidden urns,
containing ashes
of dead dreams.

I survey the spilled ashes of hopes
and find no answers
to the questions that
have thirsted away for want of answers
as to why...

I think the questions may
emerge again
when I know the schedules...
and the answers as to
my being's being,
then my soul,
my heart and I
will soar once more...
no questions asked.

Margaret T. Gilmore
1990

Winds

I'd write a song if I could find words and
I would make music if I could write notes.
And if I could I would tell how I know
that these marvelous things make music
and songs about me...and about you.

I've heard wings make many kinds of music
for me, or about me...and about you, if you knew.
Winds have moaned with me, when I've been broken,
and thought I'd never mend. And other times,
when my heart has been speechless, awed and
overwhelmed by love, winged things have spoken
softly, and translated words I could not say.

But for now, all I can tell, is how I wish I could
say how much music I hear in the way winds blow,
and in such sounds as the whispering whir of hummingbirds'
wings.

Such things as bees and butterflies, clouds in
the sky, crystal wind chimes in a window, rain drops
on my rooftop, all these make art in my heart. And then,
besides all these, I think I'm beginning to hear what I think
may be the sound of hundreds of sturdy angels traveling above
the clouds, winging their way to hover over me while I try to
think of words for songs I'd like to sing, if I could...about
all that's marvelous and beautiful in the place where I live.
I think those angels may already know the words and the music
to the songs I'd write if I could.

Margaret Taylor Gilmore
March 9, 2003

Wings and Things that Fly

Wings, winds, and wonderful things that fly...
Bees and butterflies and birds, and clouds in the sky.
Wind chimes and flute music, heard in the night...
Mystical sounds, such as angels in flight.

Things such as these cause my heart
to rise to meet them, and joy comes.
Then I am speechless with longing
trying to find words for a song
that I could write, if I could...
About what wings and winds mean to me.
Because these are things I wish that I had...
so to soar with thanksgiving
for such things as these.

I think of wings that can fly beyond the
bounds of earth and reach somewhere beyond the sky.
And just perhaps can take my heart and take it there.

And winds that I hear seem almost always
to be speaking especially to me...
Or...perhaps for me...Because they
always say things I cannot say...

Winds have moaned for me
when I've been broken and thought
I'd never mend. And sometimes...when a feeling
was too deep and I had no words
with which to express the thankful love
that was in my heart, I think the winds
have softly spoken for me and made it clear.

But for now all that I have...for awhile,
is my love for things with wings...
such as birds and bees and butterflies,
and my visions of a band of sturdy guardian angels
traveling with their wings between the winds...
singing as they come to hover over me.

Margaret Taylor Gilmore
October 4, 2002

Bells

An early morning train was rumbling through our part of town. I have become accustomed to trains going by. Over time they have become like familiar friends and their warning whistles and the sound of their wheels no longer disturb my sleep.

Sitting, listening with my cup of coffee, I was thinking how I have become able to discern by its sounds whether the cars are empty or heavily loaded. On this particular morning as the train went by, I began to hear another sound that was faint. I thought at first it must be my imagination...what I heard was like a tinkling of tiny fragile bells.

I began to listen more intently, astonished that I could hear the bells even with the train rumbling by. Then I detected the direction from which I was hearing the unusual sound.

On the top-most shelf above where I was sitting, I had placed a set of eight fragile crystal glasses. Somehow the train's rumbling wheels had caused the house to shift just enough to move the glasses so they were touching each other, moving musically to the rhythms of the rumbling wheels of the train going by.

Those glasses had not been off that shelf for months, and many trains have come past, but not until this morning had they moved to make those delicate, bell-like sounds.

For several days my mood had been somber. At the sound of delicate bells my thoughts shifted to wonder and awe and thankfulness. Because of the sound of gentle bells I am reminded that sometimes mysteriously beautiful things happen and we are reassured. Now as I think about those two sounds, it was as if I heard a today song with a lovely descant that took my heart and helped it soar heavenward.

Perhaps it isn't such a mystery after all. Because I do believe I heard reassuring music and it reminded me that wonderful things can happen to the heart on days such as this, when crystal glasses can be moved by fragments of time, to ring like bells...Simply by the rumbling of heavy wheels going by...moving closer can sometimes inspire a new song to be composed in the heart. It can happen when a person's heart is moved by an unexpected moment that enables them to move...and even by only one-minute space, but are then able to touch and be touched by...something, or someone and the heavenly bells begin to ring with gladness...somewhere.

Margaret Taylor Gilmore
October 4, 2003

A Plea for Understanding Love

"Perfect Love"

Love.
What is love?
A longing to be loved.
Perfect love must meet love
before love between two loves
can be perfected.

Perfection?
What is perfection?
Perfection is love without
reservations, without flaws...
Flaws cannot cause reservations
if love is strong enough
to see beyond the flaw
to the perfection that lies
beyond the human imperfection,
and loves without reservation.
Perfect love is all forgiving and
worthy of the love of the
perfect love of God.

Our prayer: "To perfectly love thee and worthily magnify His Holy Name." Who of us can perfectly love? Who is worthy to magnify God Almighty, the Creator of all worlds?

What IS love? Who CAN love perfectly? Love, I think, is a holy mystery we keep trying to solve.

Lord, if I am unable to love thee perfectly, then please, I pray, will you still love me in my imperfection, and teach me how to love thee and others in the way that is perfect for me?

Margaret Taylor Gilmore
April 21, 2000

It's Alright to Cry

It was a day of packing up belongings...and memories. It was a day of leaving a place I had called home for thirty years. It was a day of lifting heavy objects and of deciding what to keep and what to give away. And what would fit into a smaller house.

I had thought I would "ride off into the sunset" some day, from that lovely house, but fate decreed differently. My friends were there to help me clean out closets and remove the chandelier from over the dining room table.

The years I'd spent in that house had been some of the most challenging, demanding, perilous, exciting, and happiest of my life. I was facing the day when I was about to pull up the roots of my heart's collection of symbols of the days and nights of laughter, love, and the most demanding and most important deciding moments that had made my life an exciting and wonderful experience.

In that house I had been ecstatic with joy and brought low with weeping and sorrow. The house contained ghosts of memories of moments that in the passing years I had secretly celebrated as precious anniversaries. Suddenly I was overwhelmed with sadness. Without warning, tears began to flow. I have always tried to remain calm and meet emotionally charged moments with dignity. But that day I was unable to disguise what my heart was saying and my friends saw my tears.

The husband of my friend is a pastor. And what he said to me at that moment became an example of what one person can say that can make a difference for the rest of a lifetime. At that moment I felt as if someone had struck a stone of lonely sadness and regret in me, and liberating water of hope and faith began to flow into my very soul.

"It's alright to cry," my friend said. "Everybody has a right to cry sometimes. My wife and I cry every time we have moved. It's alright to cry. God understands."

So now I know that it is true. Jesus wept because He was sad, but also glad...because His heart knew of something wonderful that was yet to come. Today, in this new place, I am content because I have discovered that all my precious memories have moved with me into this lovely new old house.

Sometimes now, there are moments when my tears fall because I am filled with joy, and I know that's alright too.

Margaret Taylor Gilmore
On Leaving Hasell Street in Charleston, South Carolina

Love, A Word

Having had a great deal of time during the past weeks to think about what I have gleaned from having lived into the years the Bible counts as "borrowed time," I feel a need to put into words some of the thoughts that have dominated my prayers and my memories. This perhaps, is my word of farewell and welcome...

First, no matter how hard I have tried...I have not solved many of life's mysteries. I have now, at this age, more questions than answers as to how to explain the events of my lifetime. I have lived my life in a manner I have described as "Spiritual Braille." And now, at this point I continue to do so, because faith is a moment to moment exercise. Life is full of surprises. The only explanation I can discern is that there is an almighty being who holds the world and every living creature in His hands, and we are not meant to be able to see the future He has ordained for us as individuals or for the world's destiny. That He loves us is the ultimate truth.

Living by spiritual Braille has enabled me to find light on the path of my life, and strength of mind and body to be a willing, even eager pilgrim, keeping my soul's eyes on the distant Grail. The light draws me, and my trust enables me to follow.

Lately I have remembered people, events and experiences...And I have remembered not just Biblical promises, but paragraphs from books I have read. Long forgotten "gems" have surfaced and have helped me through this time of testing.

James Weldon Johnson has written something about death in his book, *"God's Trombones."* In one of the chapters he has described the final hour in the life of an elderly woman. He says: *"She turned her head and saw what we could not see. She saw old Death a'coming, and he looked to her like a welcome friend."* Many times recently I have turned my head and waited to welcome death who would arrive to escort me home...perhaps an angel, or Jesus Himself...a welcome friend.

A part of a popular song from the years of World War II echoes in the background of my thoughts...as a sort of descant to my prayers as I recall relationships that remain, strangely significant, no matter how brief, how long, they were. *"We'll meet again, don't know where, don't know when, but I know we'll meet again some sunny day..."* As I think of those words, those individuals, I wonder who, where and when...in this world or in the next...that reunion will take place...but I am distinctly encouraged. I recall hands clasped, I am comforted at remembrance of strong embraces and words that were lasting covenants, sturdy anchors throughout many years.

And those remembered encounters create for me today a mounting awareness of an all-consuming LOVE...and a clearer interpretation of who Jesus was...IS...

As I contemplate all the individuals who come to my mind...those in my past and in my present, the word LOVE is overwhelming. I am brought to my knees by an emotion of longing to make all of them know of the enduring LOVE that engulfs my soul as I count them, one by one...They know who they are...those whom I have loved and those who have loved me...Now, as I consider the deepest desire of my heart it is that knowing I love them still...will become a source of gentle reassurance to them all. Family, friends, fellow pilgrims, acquaintances, students, strangers I have met for a very brief time (who may have been angels) wherever you are, I have not forgotten. Each time there came into being a unique and mutually enriching sharing of our spirits.

As I go through this time of uncertainly, my physical strength seemingly gradually draining away, I continue to plead with the Holy Spirit for guidance as to how to meet the coming days. The instinctive desire of my heart is that I be permitted to recover and to finish certain goals I have set for myself. But the word LOVE dominates my thoughts as I consider the question...what IS, what ARE the primary desires of my heart?

A strange analogy has come to me as I have prayed for an answer to my questions as to how, when and how much more of an active life God has prepared for me. I begin to identify with Jesus, who loved without reservation. The desire of His heart was to make it clear to everyone that the sovereign God wanted nothing more than that individuals would accept the fact that they were LOVED.

I am brought to tears as I realize one of the deepest desires of my heart is to somehow make certain that all the people who through the years have been a significant part, for long periods or in brief encounters will be assured that not a one of them has been forgotten. Not just remembered, but prayed for as they come to my mind. It has become very important to me, as I look to the time when I will become a part of the ages, that all of you, somehow, will believe, as I do, that by some means in this life or in the next, that we will meet again.

Our connection, forged by the Holy Spirit, was sealed at the moment our eyes met. Our relationship from that moment had a unique and timeless meaning and purpose. LOVE entered our lives in a way none of us were aware of at that moment...and will never fully comprehend. A first glance, and we were forever linked. Some of those unexpected meetings became precious relationships that have enabled us to grow closer as we kept in touch...Others, seemingly too brief to be of importance, are worked into the tapestry of the pattern of our lives and we have not been fully aware of how lasting and how long-lasting for good...was the impact of that brief encounter to our lives. LOVE sometimes reveals itself to us as a rainbow. Sometimes it comes to us disguised as something very ordinary...as if it were a convenient circumstance.

That LOVE, destined by God, remains an eternal element that links us. Just as Jesus' eyes met the eyes of others, some felt the divinity in the experience, and were forever changed by that look of LOVE, this is how I believe the holy mystery of divine LOVE came into our lives when my eyes met yours...and you are one of those whom I now anticipate I will meet again... some sunny day.

For whatever it may mean today, tomorrow, or in months or years to come, as long as I continue to breathe God's healing breath, I write this paper to attempt to sort out my own spiritual healing...My "spiritual Braille" has urged me to put these thoughts into visible availability.

If I am near to the day of my death, let these words be affirmation that I believe in God's eternal LOVE and I enter tomorrow, here or in heaven, trusting in Jesus' words, "Believe also in Me." If, through the experiences of physical discomfort of late has given me a deeper, clearer concept of discernment more of how Jesus felt as he attempted to personify God's LOVE...and thus has made me a more prepared individual to help others to know more of LOVE...I thank you, Lord God.

If there is more for me to learn, to teach, to be an example, so be it. For God has surrounded me throughout these many years with individuals for me to love and treasure, and I look forward to meeting you all...again...some sunny day. Thanks be to God for mysteries, for people to love and blessings beyond measure...

Margaret Taylor Gilmore
March 6, 1998

"A Lady Alone" by Alice Ward

Personal

What Do I Do Now, God?

What do I do now, God? I have used all the hours you gave me. I have spent all the time you gave me to invest. At least up to this hour.

I am wondering God. I have watched, I have listened. I have waited, and I have wondered what it was I was waiting for. I have tried, and I have thought I made progress. I have tried, and I thought I failed. But was it progress, and was it failure? Who can I ask, God? Who will know? Who would understand my questions?

I have loved, and I have tried to express that love in all the ways I understood, and I have always wondered if anything I did was really RIGHT...really all I should do...and never knew how to make it any more...or any righter...

I have always wondered. I have wondered about myself, and what it is that I was supposed to have done with my life. I have invested my life, my time, myself...into whatever seemed called for, appropriate at the time. Whatever, wherever I have been I have felt as though I have been sincere in my efforts to be all that I could be then and there. Honestly sincere.

I wonder now, what has it all counted for? And as the end of the play approaches, and I know the cue for the curtain is bound to be not many years away, I listen to my memories, and they are interesting, but I wonder what the plot of the play was about. Have I missed something I should have seen...or heard?

In my role in the time-frame into which I was born...was I a star? Was I a full participant in my generation's play, or was I a walk-on, and walk-off? And was I worthy of my assigned role, my calling? Or did I miss something important somewhere along my way, and am I forever lost in meaninglessness?

If I missed a cue, when was it? Where was it? Who gave it? Right now I am not sure if I am still listed in the cast, or am I now just watching from the wings, until the end?

If the final curtain were to fall today, God...would there be applause? I hope so...I would like to believe there would be recognition and welcome and rejoicing, and at least a few, "well dones"...(And I'd find him and say, "How'd I do, Grandpa?" because he's the one I promised I'd meet him again one day...)

What do I do now, God? Thinking about it...I think I will wait, as I always have done, for the great director. I like to think about the firmament and a background of eternity. God knows about those things. I like to think about that kind of a beginning for...my ending...

Margaret Taylor Gilmore
September 1, 1981

Experiencing Bliss

It is said that when time, place and purpose are in perfect balance together, that awesome and wonderfully soul fulfilling emotions are likely to happen. It is as if in surprised amazement one would say, "Wow...that's it...I've experienced the most thrilling and unforgettable moment of my life." This is the kind of experience people pray for, study for, wait for, work for, long for, and sometimes not knowing why, there are people who even kill for, in the hope that perhaps through a violent act some thrilling moment of all knowingness will come.

But truly perfect moments do not come because one deliberately arranges them. We do not make them out of ourselves, they are from being caught up in times when we are in a place for a purpose that allows a sense of the holy to take charge of our knowingness.

The writer, Joseph Campbell, spent his lifetime studying the history of people of every era, over all the world, to learn how and when and if...they have all longed for a special moment when they experience a kind of perfect "bliss." This is more than happiness, it is a spiritual enlightenment. Once having known bliss, Campbell believed an individual becomes thereafter a more complete person. And that knowingness is of God.

Life cannot be lived in one long state of blissfulness, but there can be times when we become so totally present in the perfect moment in which we find ourselves ...that...an ineffable bliss overtakes us. That is when we become more prepared to gradually become the individual we are born to be. Then we are forever after able to see, hear, know, understand the meaning of joy and more of who and what we really are. Until then we are not aware of what it is we are longing to experience, we sense only that we need to know something. The soul knows that it longs to know a moment that can define perfection...it is the nearest one can get to a fulfillment of knowing perfection. In such awesome moments we may see ourselves in a reflection of God's perfect love.

One of my most blissful moments came during Christmas week several years ago. I was invited to a large ranch home in Colorado. The house was filled with all the wonderful sacred symbols of the season, and there was festive music and food, and guests in formal attire. Some people sang with the music, others gathered in more quiet rooms to talk and laugh together. It was a clear and star lit night and a rare privilege to celebrate the season in such an elegant old place.

When it was time for us to go home, my friends and I stood at the door waiting for an attendant to bring our car. All of a sudden there came a tremendous sound of hundreds of wings overhead, and Canada Geese calling triumphantly as they landed on the lake just across the road from where we stood. They had followed a trusted leader on a long journey and had reached their destination. We smiled at each other...awed at the thrill of such an unexpected experience. The geese rejoicing voices made us feel as if we were united in joy, celebrating something amazingly wonderful, as if in those moments they belonged to us and we to them. We were surprised by joy.

And it had begun to snow again. Great swirls of huge flakes soon covered us, but we stood still, transfixed and in awe of the moment we were a part of. Behind us was the sound of Christmas music, and filtered through the falling snow were the misty, multicolored outside lights of Christmas.

Those were magical moments and the three of us have never forgotten...I have often thought how filled with symbolic beauty was that night and those birds. It was an experience filled with an emotion that is difficult to describe. I think of no other word than bliss. And remembering that night we have become even more aware that we were blessed. We were in a perfect place at a perfect moment to celebrate, in a rare and remarkable way, a perfect event.

Since that night we have become aware that we have an increased capacity for reverence for the sights and sounds of earth's bounty, more awed and thankful for the generosity of the love that created Christmas. Because we experienced a moment of bliss, on a Christmas night that was especially holy unto us.

Margaret Taylor Gilmore
September 1, 2002

Afterglow

Now I am silent at the sight
of burning bushes,
flaming trees,
glowing embers.
I am quiet
as I observe,
Remembering...
events of my life
that had flamed and burned,
then at an autumn time became
only fondly remembered glowing embers.

They were my life's own
enriching, enlightening fires,
that warmed in me in springtimes
in autumns and in the winters
of my life.
Now memory is the blessing
that warms me. And I know that
sometime, somewhere,
I will know why and when and how
I will also become a remembered
warmth.

And now it is the sight
of wisps of silver clouds and moons
wandering together across the sky
that cause me to recall flaming
fires and the peace that glowed
within my heart when I first saw
a bush that burned and tree aflame...

Now I am warmed, remembering
the joy, the quiet reassurance
that blessed my life within those flames
of mine, that were so brief, so everlasting.

Margaret Taylor Gilmore
November 26, 1999

Burning Bushes

I've seen bushes burning this year,
sometimes they were small sparks of red,
scarlet vines twined in branches
or gnarled old trees.
Like bright necklaces they draped
along tree limbs, like border trim
on a lady's leaf-green dress.

Sometimes I have seen glistening
scarlet blazing from a low bush, a small,
common weed that by autumn's touch
had become a ruby royalty.

Once, filtered by an evening's dying light
I saw one unforgettable glorious sight...
A young, perfectly shaped maple tree
aflame, glowing blood red, every leaf
engulfed entirely by autumn.

Margaret Taylor Gilmore
November 26, 1995

Pea Ridge Reunion

There is a quiet place on a gentle mound, not quite lofty enough to be called a hill, where ancient trees bend protectively over one special space nearest the road. And across from it, along a lower level, a little stream runs past.

Lying beneath the trees are graves of men who died in a battle many years ago. I have written of it, because to me it is a sacred place.

My mother's grave is there, marked by a modest stone. Once, several years ago, after many years had passed, I walked there, searching for the spot my mother shares among many others. I had wondered how I would feel when I found it. And when I stood there, what I felt was not sadness. It was as if I heard her quietly say, "Well, I knew you'd come someday."

My mother was in her early twenties when she died. I was four years old, and today I am a great grandmother. I have often wondered, when we meet in heaven, how will we recognize each other? Shortly after she died, my father and his parents took me many miles from where I was born, and many years have passed since the day my mother was buried on that hill.

Perhaps if I trace my thoughts from the beginning, I will find some connective paths as to why I feel so connected to the story of the Battle of Rea Ridge. I will begin again:

Beneath the sheltering trees on a little hill is a spot, chosen long ago for graves of men who died in a Civil War battle fought near the town. In the years since, a larger area was set aside for graves of other people, many of whom are descendants of the soldiers buried there.

A peacefulness permeates the atmosphere. I saw the place in late summer when the little mound that is not quite a hill, was still green, but I could tell already that in autumn it would become gloriously gold. One can stand there, and in the distance view Pea Ridge where a mighty battle was fiercely fought many years ago. It isn't far away, and the day I walked on the grounds where the battle was fought, I thought I could almost hear, in the windy silence that blows across the ridges, faint moans, like an aching sadness that lingers there, too deep to describe.

People of the town point out the house, still standing, that was the home of a young woman who was engaged to be married to one of the soldiers who died during the battle of Pea Ridge. The story is told that when battle was over, the young woman took a wagon and drove a team of horses to the ridge to find her lover's body. Finding it, she laid him to rest in the soft green earth they dug that day for a grave on the peaceful little hill.

Today the spot where he lies with other men who died in the birth pangs of early America, is officially designated as historically significant, and it has been carefully tended throughout the years.

Now I think I know what...,who...why the place continues to call me, after all these many years... I believe it is the echo of deathless faith that was in the heart of that girl woman who searched through a field of dead men to find her loved one. I believe she believed there would be a someday when they would meet again, all wounds healed.

And, like her, I believe in a heavenly physician who can erase from our memory all human flesh and can preserve the spirit part of us that is timeless and ageless. I believe someday everyone will see exactly who we were when our human eyes first saw each other, at any age of our earthly lives.

I have a feeling that women, especially...will rejoice one day for many reasons, and even perhaps for some, there will be angels ringing wedding bells for couples who may have been parted on earth for awhile, because the men died fighting for their causes and country, and to protect the women they loved.

And I always smile when I remember lines I once heard spoken by a man whose mother had died: "The gates swung wide, the angels sang, Saint Peter smiled, and in walked my Mom." I like to think..."My Mom, too"...

Contemplating today my emotions when I found the small head stone on which is carved my mother's name, and read the words, "Christ in me, the hope of glory", I think I may have glimpsed a vision of a time when my mother and I will meet and she will greet me with motherly love and perhaps she will say, "Well, I knew you'd get here some time."

And perhaps there will come a time when Pea Ridge winds will sing again of peace on earth.

Margaret Taylor Gilmore
August 29, 2005

"Lady at the Table" by Alice Ward

Old Testament Meditations

The Beginning of the Beginning

Growing more and more inspired, God saw more of the emerging possibilities and He began dividing the waters to make earth spaces for places where grasses and trees could grow and where beasts and birds could live in mutual enjoyment.

Then, after that, God sat down to rest awhile from his creating. He looked at the sun and the moon, and the waters and the mountains. He looked on all the living trees and grasses and the creatures He had made and He smiled. "I have made a place fit for my angels to enjoy. Now I can observe my work and see how well its creatures live together...I feel a great satisfaction at what I have made. Now I can watch it all thrive and grow and see seasons come and go.

"With all this, if I wish, I can drink of the water, and I can taste the richness of the grains and the sweetness of the fruits of the trees. I have made a beautiful garden place, and I am glad in it. I think I will call it Eden." And God walked in His garden and was glad.

God smiled, angels sang thankful songs and little brooks rippled, making sounds that God called music. Multitudes of birds sang and soft dews caressed the grasses every morning, great sea animals splashed and made huge waves in their wake.

God was satisfied and He loved it all. Then He began to feel something else was needed. "I want to share this wonderful place," He said to himself. And for a while He pondered. Then one morning just as the sun began to rise, He said, "I know what I will do...I'll create a man...I'll make someone somewhat like me, who will feel love for this earth and its beauty and bounty as much as I do..."

Then God knelt down by a sparkling stream and began scooping up hands full of damp clay. He let His imagination do what it had inspired Him to do during all those hours while He was creating the earth, a day at a time.

First He carefully rounded out a ball of clay, just enough to fill His two hands, then He made another, larger ball. He placed them together, then He made four small lumps, placing them in the palms of His hand, and He rolled each of them into almost equally similar lengths. These He attached evenly to the larger lump. These became two arms, two legs, and at the end of each pair, He carefully added hands and feet.

Then, with exceeding care, He began sculpting a face into the first round ball. Slowly and gently, He intricately detailed the image. Now and then He reshaped a brow, a lip, an ear, stopping and starting again, rearranging parts and pieces. Once, contemplating what else would be needed here or there, he smoothed it out and started over. It took a while, but finally He knew it was His best work. It was the finest, most beautiful thing He had made.

He waited a while, and then when the clay was firm, but still a bit damp, God held His masterpiece close to His heart, lovingly, for it was His first son. Then, like one breathing into someone's lungs breath from their own body, the Lord God Almighty breathed into the man He had formed out of clay, and Adam's lungs were filled with the breath of life. And then God smiled and Adam stood up, cupped his hands together and drank deeply from the clear and sunlit river water running at his feet.

Out of the darkness of nothing, came someone...From out of somewhere in eternity came the one whose beginning remains a mystery, but whose creation in the beginning remains entirely visible. He whose breath of life He gave to Adam, still He gives to us, and still provides the fruit of the grains and the trees to give us strength.

Each springtime, each Easter reminds us that breath to breath, moment to moment, each one of us still share today in the gift of the breath of Him who created a garden of glory. We are reminded that in His longing to share good things, Adam was God's first masterpiece, and in expressing His love, He also sent Jesus to us.

Easter reminds us of God's ultimate gift...life after death. And as we sit together to share a meal with family or friends, it makes the moment and the food more blessed as we reflect on the fact that every morsel we eat proves that something has died so that we might live. Then we remember thankfully that we have been nourished by a someone who has never abandoned His creations.

Margaret Taylor Gilmore
April 4, 2002

Genesis

Carefully and meticulously, the record keepers recorded the genealogies. Such diligence, we believe, was according to God's plan, else why would such long lists of names have lasted so exactly for so long a time?

Somehow all these names must be important for us to know. All the unpronounceable names and all the different clans and the tribes and where they lived make difficult reading.

Some facts, tucked in among the lists of names are bits and pieces of additional information, such as the note in Chapter 10, Verse 9, where we read, "Nimrod, who grew to be a mighty warrior in the earth."

There are notations of clans within the nations, each with its own language. (Chapter 10, Verse 4) But later, in Chapter 11, we are told that everyone spoke the same language.

Chapter 10 contains a history of the descendants of Noah's sons. This appears to cover at least three generations. Many events took place, many children were born.

Many people tell me they skip over all those parts of the chapters that are mostly lists. I have found that reading every word, every name is excellent mental discipline. For it is easy to read and not read at all, because the mind is off on another track of thought, even as we read lines of uninteresting copy. I have learned to "master my mind" to better attention to dull details and have discovered interesting bits and pieces of information like that line about Nimrod.

I have friends who are deep into research into family genealogies. They are absorbed in the search for these same, small scraps of information that give hints of larger sources to find more of the people of their family lineage. These may be people who might never have been remembered at all by anyone and this fellow who "was a son of the son of the son"...of someone whose name connects, and the history of the family is more complete than before.

As I grow older, I find I become increasingly interested to know more about my own ancestors. Today I am thinking perhaps those long dead people are somewhere, waiting to be remembered and called by their name.

Reading I am thinking about who might I find if I were to tackle a research to "get in touch" with my earlier kin. Then I thought, "We are all kin." Because before all those sons of Noah had all those sons and daughters, there was a couple, Adam and Eve, and all of those families, clans, tribes, and nations who were the children of the children born in Eden.

I am a descendant of Hugh Johnson Taylor and Margaret Robbins Taylor. Before that I have no records. Margaret died young and Hugh married Alice. She bore no children, but she is the only paternal grandmother I ever knew. And I loved her, but I doubt I ever told her so.

John Earl Taylor was Hugh Taylor's youngest son. He was my father. Gladys Irene Fair Taylor, my mother, was a daughter of Joseph and Susan Fair. I am kin to the Kelly's by way of my mother's sisters, three of whom married Kelly's. I wish I knew more about the people from whom I inherited my genes.

And will I be known and will I know them when I reach the place where all generations finally go. And are they already aware that I am thinking of them? "Good morning, Grandma, good morning, Grandpa Taylor!"

Bless us, Lord, as we reach back and as we reach forward to find who we are and who You are...and bless us as we attempt to express the awe and the wonder at the mystery that has brought us thus far...together.

Margaret Taylor Gilmore

Questions I've Asked the Voice Within

The voice within me persists in asking questions. Why do I feel compelled to make record of those questions? Will I find answers sometime? And will it matter if I find them? If so...then with whom should I share my asking and the answers? I begin by asking why do I think I need to know answers to questions my mind asks? For example: Who wrote the Book of Genesis?

Did the world begin and earth start with one speck of something from somewhere too distant to discern with eyes like ours, but clearly seen by the creator of worlds? And what were the elements in that lump of clay that became a man? And from what origin language was drawn his name, Adam?

And perhaps might the creation story in the Book of Genesis have been told by Adam to whom the creator spoke, saying "Listen, I am your God, I made you a man. I exist within your physical body and in the deepest depths of your mind. I will always be with you. I will speak with you today to tell you what you are to do to fulfill your life's purpose. Now listen carefully, Adam, because this is my voice, speaking into the deepest part of your thoughts. You are to remember and relate to your offspring all you have seen of the way I have created the world, and have enabled you to understand."

I wonder...was Adam faithful to his calling? And did he always remember to rely on the voice within as he became a husband and father to two boys? At mealtimes, did Adam and Eve teach them garden wisdom, and did they not warn their sons it is a dangerous thing to disobey the rules God makes?

Did Adam and Eve also sometimes hear other voices, just as we do? Those voices from other sources that can crowd into our mind and cause us to be anxious, asking, longing, doubting, and threaten to steal the peace and purpose from our soul?

How many years did Adam and Eve live? And how many times did Adam attempt to describe to his children the strange event when he knew he was a new kind of being...and something within him told him he was a man person?

And did Adam and Eve grow old physically just as we do? And did they ever wonder why did age have to come as a puzzling, surprising experience? And when they died, was there already a heaven somewhere?

Even though Adam and Eve must have had times when they wondered, and their faith may have wavered when their son Cain killed his brother Able, I believe they both died in peace, because the voice that spoke that morning when they were both so very new...never stopped reminding both of them saying, "I am your God. You are mine, I created you and you will always matter to me. Therefore, I will never forsake you."

Now I wonder why I wonder. This morning after writing these lines, I have heard a voice within speaking, "Trust me. I created you and you are mine. I will never forsake you."

Now I am thinking that Genesis is a story still evolving. Our world is still being created. And the Father of Adam remains in charge of the ongoing of it all, because He loves all He has created. Today I have decided I do not need to know all the answers to how God made the world. It is enough to be reminded of how much we matter to Him.

Margaret Taylor Gilmore
July 1, 2005

God's Growth and Yours and Mine

In my search for what a good friend once called "water from deeper wells", a thought has come to me concerning who God was at the beginning, who He is today, and who I was and now am, because I am made in His image.

Reading Genesis, the God I find is the great I Am. Too vast a being to be described and at that point, too vague to be real to the concept of my human mind.

But I sense a great hovering, I sense a pensive being whose mind was like that of an artist whose thoughts began to churn with color and design and He began to create shapes and textures, putting them together in His hands. And gradually by His thinking of what could be, there was a world and then there was a beautiful garden, and a man and a woman. Perfectly made, they were endowed with personalities and intellects to fit perfectly into that perfect place. And God was happy, and they were loved.

And God surveyed His world and saw that it was a good and beautiful thing He had made. This was the beginning. And on one of the first days in the garden, the creator became a voice and He spoke to the man and the woman asking questions a parent would ask.

But, sadly, by the time the two people had become too numerous a people to count, most of them had become thoughtless and ungrateful for the wonderful world God had made.

By the time historians began to keep records of the succession of the kings they had insisted they wanted, it became abundantly evident that God was becoming very disappointed at the way His people were ignoring Him and even worse, they were worshiping gods they had made with their own hands. Time after time, God forgave and rescued them from their folly, but even after that, the people were prone to return to the "high places" to worship gods they believed would give them physical blessings.

Hopefully, the creator of the world sent chosen individuals into the midst of the people, warning them He was displeased...even angry. This was a new, unwelcome and unfamiliar emotion for God, and it caused Him to be not only angry, it made Him sad.

The books of the Kings contain seemingly endless accounts of evil, deception, violence, and the oceans of blood that was shed by thousands of individuals, caught up in the wars that seemed never to end. Time after time, the God who watched all this sent prophets and priests to warn the kings of His increasing sorrow...for He had become exceedingly angry.

The being, who had caused the earth to emerge, had by now become a larger presence and gradually, like a loving parent, increasingly sad because His world was no longer a lovely place. And worst of all, His children did not regard Him with appreciation, but worshiped idols they made themselves.

God intervened with mighty acts and caused kings to kill each other and their armies to kill everyone and destroy everything in their paths...And kill they did. By the thousands upon thousands, people were slaughtered. God had become someone very different from the inspired artist who built a peaceful Eden for two people.

Now God dealt with individuals, and collectively with large numbers of people. Now and then He sent a certain individual with whom He had spoken, giving them power to speak for Him, He enabled them to work miracles to demonstrate His power to protect and forgive if they would forsake their worship of false gods. God was the one God, and His heart had been broken time after time. He was no longer the gentle keeper of a safe garden. His anger burned fiercely across whole kingdoms, killing entire thousands of armies and hundreds of people in their paths.

God created himself, generation by generation. He made us for Himself and we are like Him. Does it not follow that we are like Him as we gradually become more and more aware of Him, he becomes increasingly more REAL? Gradually we begin to feel the presence of Christ within, and day by day, we find that He understands us personally, and He walks beside us because He made us to be like Him. And so...together we continue to create the bonds of our kinship.

And when we acknowledge Him, all nature sings for us as if we are in Eden. And God smiles.

"Lead on, O thy Eternal...some of us will follow...trusting You to lead us through the years to the Promised Land."

Margaret Taylor Gilmore
July 15, 2001

God's Breath

God scooped up a handful of clay and when he had formed it into the first human being ever made, then he breathed on what he had made and Adam's lungs received the life-giving air and God's breath nurtured every drop of blood that began to flow through Adam's body.

Thus began the miracle that happens, moment to moment, day by day, year by year to every one of us. As we breathe in the life-giving breath of God, our lungs are filled with sustaining strength to carry God's nurturing presence into every single drop of blood that flows through our body.

As in us, God's breath moves all the world in consistent rhythms. His breath causes the tides to rise and fall. And it is his breath that is in the winds that blow. We are created to be dependent on God's breath to keep us alive, and it takes only a few minutes in an airless room to make us keenly aware of how much we depend on the availability of renewing, restorative air.

To consciously take note as we take a breath and think how our entire body is built to depend on air, and how it responds each time our lungs receive another measure of life is to be reminded of the power that is the breath of God and the source of all miracles.

Breathe on me, breath of God...Fill me with fresh faith, life and love and your peace, enough to share...today.

Margaret Taylor Gilmore
December 3, 2001

A Prayer for Double Portions

II Kings to Chapter 10

This book moves swiftly through the events that marked the life of the Prophet Elisha. There is much to indicate that indeed, Elisha had been given "a double portion" of the gifts that had been those of his mentor, Elijah. Both were powerful men whose "connection" with the true God was well-known, feared and respected.

Imagery found in these chapters, mirror similar events that take place in previous chapters and in other books of the Old Testament...and they foreshadow events that are recorded in the New Testament. Several similar themes, similar situations, mark significant events in the old and new eras.

Miracles and foreknowledge, healing, triumphs in warfare, multiplication of resources...appear in the record of Elisha's years of influence...as in the case of the widow who needed money to pay off debts so that she could save her sons from being sold as slaves...can be recognized as similar to those in other books about other individuals.

According to the counsel of Prophets, many kings went to war each spring to successfully capture more lands for their people and their animals. But there is treachery, bribery, murder and all manner of the thread of evil that runs throughout the checkered history of God's chosen people.

There is evidence of a strange (perhaps not so strange) mindset of those ancient people. Many believed in the God of Israel and they feared His power, but they also feared and worshipped other gods as well (and so do we today).

Not many of those early kings were admirable people. Most "Did evil in the sight of the Lord," and the prophets warned them frequently at the peril of their lives.

Did Elisha's double portion make him a more successful, effective prophet? One can imagine that his asking for a double portion indicated he had visions of doing great and mighty things for his people...but it sounds as if frustration and anger were his emotions many times. Still there were those who observed, believed and obeyed the ancient laws. Perhaps that "double portion" was what kept alive that flickering flame of love for the Lord's chosen people that had once burned brightly in the prophet's heart, but was heavy with sadness. Who knows?

Margaret Taylor Gilmore
April 20, 1996

New Psalms to Sing

Reading the Book of Psalms is to me like listening to a great orchestra playing a composition written by an inspired artist.

As I read, I am caught up in visualizations of Eden-like places. Then, reading further, I find my thoughts rebelling against the descriptive darkness of corruption, greed, and cruelty endured by helpless people. I rejoice in reading of the pleasures and I regret the sad plights of the history of Abraham's children. I hear echoes of those years as the story in music rises and falls, as is so beautifully expressed songs written by David.

When life was good, greed grew stronger. When life was easy, the people tended to forget the years when their lives had been so very hard. We wonder how they could so quickly forget that the Lord had answered their prayers for forgiveness and always rescued them when they were in deep distress.

I sometimes read David's Psalms with a prayer for some small phrase or promise to carry into my day, a little like some good luck charm. I search for a thought I can remember throughout the day. And I never fail to come upon a verse that is like a reassuring affirmation that God heard my request.

Many of the Psalms are credited to David, whose life was a symbolic musical score. The history of his life inspired themes for many songs he wrote during those remarkable experiences. Even though David's life was more dramatic than most of ours, his words express emotions familiar to most of us. They are very similar to the same highs and the lows, the loves and the losses most of us have known.

His songs describe depths of pain and passion and of regret and of his moments of awe and reverence. David sometimes indicated the instruments that should make the music to match the mood of his songs. His sensitivity is exceedingly evident. That is why his Psalms sometimes sound like moans of regret and pleas for balm from Gilead. Some of his songs make us meditative as we recognize the depth of his regret and sadness. Sometimes we hear reverent gladness in his expressions of heart quivering, quiet thankfulness.

Then come the haunting memory songs of a history forgotten and the ultimate terrors and despair that David expressed in words set to music and played to the wailing moans of horns played by people who remembered regretfully and were deeply sad. But always there are his affirmations of remembrance that God will always be God, and the assurance that no prayer of confession, no prayer for forgiveness is beyond the hearing of The Almighty. And there are passages when the heavenly music overwhelms the poet's power to describe. Every rich and royal sound the earth can make, and every melody the stars can sing combine to celebrate the promise of a peace that is beyond understanding. All this David wrote about and set to music.

Every early morning as I read and pray I become more ready to meet the day with its inevitable decisions I will have to make. David has reminded us that God is always present and with my heart prepared, I open my door to welcome the world, prepared to make music out of whatever God has for me to do, say, write, be...on this...another day He has given me. I will rejoice today and be glad in it.

Margaret Taylor Gilmore
January 8, 2005

David at Dawn

In Psalm 57, I see in my imagination David, having risen just before dawn, sitting outside his tent gazing toward the east where the sun will soon rise. He is strumming softly on his harp while his prayers rise with the music.

He prays, "Have mercy on me, O God, have mercy on me, for in You my soul takes refuge. I will take refuge in the shadow of your wings until the disaster has passed." In the next lines David meditates on the might and the numbers of his enemy and confesses he is "bound down in distress."

But his thoughts return to his faith and he sings softly, "My heart is steadfast, O God, my heart is steadfast. I will sing and make music. Awake my soul, awake harp and lyre. I will awake the dawn. I will sing of You among the people, for great is Your love that reaches to the heavens. Your faithfulness reaches to the sky."

I see David going back to his tent and his companions, his heart strengthened and his face resolute. In those dark hours of the night, before the sun rose, David had been struggling with worry, wondering how and where the enemy would attack him next. But now the sun had risen over the hills and in its light had come David's remembrance of how many times in the past he had already experienced rescue and success...and the knowledge that solution and safety had come, not because he was a perfect man or that he had the greatest army to fight for him, but because he remembered that nothing is impossible with God.

And so, David faced his fears and God reassured him. The enemy was still there, but David was no longer without hope. The next several Psalms describe David's thoughts on how God would deal with the evil men who were pursuing him. Verse 5 of Psalm 65 says, "You answer us (our people) with awesome deeds of righteousness, God, our Savior."

In the light of the terrible event that happened in New York recently, I find David's Psalms to be exceedingly encouraging. Those words he composed at a time of threatening, fearful, uncertainty in his life remind me of how many times God has arranged my feet so that I could walk safely through my own dangerous paths during those dark nights of my soul...And not mine only, but for America.

Margaret Taylor Gilmore
September 2001

Have We Built Our Towers too Tall?

Oh my Lord, this morning I am wondering...
Is the tower beginning to crumble?
Have we built our towers too tall,
sent our rockets too high?
Are we lacking in amazement
that we can, at any moment,
speak to anyone, if we wish,
even if they live a place
farthest from where we are?
Are we too proud of our war
machines that makes us strongest
of all the armies in the world?

Lord, we shuddered at seeing
of how suddenly disaster
struck New York,
and how dismayed we were when
our space explorers were killed
just when we thought they were safe.

Lord, have we grown too big,
too tall, too proud,
too ungrateful for blessings?
Have we forgotten to remember
exactly who enabled us to grow
so strong and so wealthy
and so free from dangers from afar...

Lord, we pray, now that
again we are at war,
we ask once more for
Your forgiveness before
we self-destruct and
become dust in the rubble
of the tower of success
we have been building
without remembering Babel,
forgetting there are limits
to Your patience when nations
fail to remember who You are.

Margaret Taylor Gilmore
March 24, 2003

Incredible

To me...the word incredible holds a vastness of amazement, and an underlying fascination that is like an invitation to dare believe in unbelievable things.

Contemplating today as I read in the Book of Psalms, I have a dawning impression that in a number of ways, I am a bit like David. And I find that idea incredible.

As I "listen" to what David has written, I get a strong impression he composed most of his songs as he prayed and then because he loved music, he decided his words needed to be sung and accompanied by instruments. He even gave instructions to the director as to which instrument was to be used with each song.

I'm thinking the way in which I am somewhat like David is because I too have learned that when I write my prayers, as I put them into actual words on paper, my thoughts tend to stay much more focused on what I am trying to express to the Almighty as I think words of praise and thanksgiving, in petition, and in intercession for others.

Before I begin to read, I ask God to "break the bread of life to me"...and I find as I read...any day, in any book of the Bible, that before I finish, I "hear" God feeding me by focusing my attention on one specific sentence or word that sheds a clearer light on a current concern and gives me a distinctly personal interpretation to what I have been reading. Even though these moments happen almost daily, I am always amazed at how specifically I find clearings in the mists of my contemplative thoughts...incredible!

And...upon further contemplation of David's Psalms, I recognize what seems to me to be sudden shifting to his thoughtful direction. Part way through a stanza, David's tone often changes from ..."I am hurting, Lord, why aren't you listening?" Then his words change, midway, to..."You are my Lord...You have always been faithful to rescue your children...I will praise You because I am confident You keep Your promise..."

It is easy to become distracted and depressed when life presents us with what appears to be too much to bear. David had a great many distractions to deal with.

David's life held the full range of experiences that test most people during the course of a lifetime. It is easy to recognize what mood was moving his emotions when he wrote each of them out in praise and petition to the Almighty. By the time he began writing the Psalms I read today, 55 and 56, David had come a long way from the boy he was when he dared challenge the giant Goliath, armed with only his slingshot and five smooth stones. Somehow, today I believe he felt more confident after he had discovered how much closer he felt to God when he began putting his prayers into song-words. Just as has happened to me.

David was a multi-talented man who lived a long time ago. But strangely...today he seems to me to be an individual I almost feel a kinship of spirit...He lived life with eager enthusiasm, gaining courage to meet whatever events a day might bring. He said in his songs that he trusted in the presence of God to protect him, lead, rescue, heal, and provide for him all that he needed. And so do I.

The giants I have had to face in life have not appeared in physical form, but have sometimes been like persistent swarms of nagging gnats that have driven me to my knees. Then from my knees, I could see God's face beyond the multiple problems and found patience to prevail, until in spite of trials and frustrations, peace returned to me.

And perhaps most incredible of all is this: I do truly believe that even though He knows the name of more people since Adam and Eve than anyone can count, I am confident God actually does know MY name. Just as He knew David's name and just as He heard David's song and prayers, I believe He listens when I pray. The joy He gives me as I wake each morning is because I know He knows I am thankful to be surrounded by His presence.

And each dawn as I read and pray and write my thoughts, I think the music that comes into my heart is like that which David heard, and it echoes through the busy moments of my day. And I think, "How unbelievably incredible!"

Margaret Taylor Gilmore
October 3, 2001

Praise for Joy-Filled Love

The closing verses of the Book of Psalms create a crescendo of joy-filled praise. "Let everything that has breath praise the Lord." This sentence sums up the message the writer has tried to express.

These words hold tremendous significance. "....everything that has breath..." Every living thing has breath. Air is essential to plants, to seeds under the ground, to clouds, to life in all its forms. Life comes from the powerful breath of God. And if God is a living, loving creator of all things, then love, received and given, is as crucial to life as air.

Unexpectedly, thinking on this, I recalled the joy-filled words of a song popular several years ago..."Ah, sweet mystery of life, at last I've found you. Ah, at last I know the secret of it all. For 'tis love and love alone the world is seeking, and 'tis love and love alone that can repay..."

The writer composed those words thinking of his beloved. They have the same meaning when applied to a spiritual, Biblical definition. The mystery of God's love in all its power and wonder is translated into joyful discovery for those who find an indescribable love in human terms.

Then one begins to comprehend, perhaps for the first time that human love is but a hint of what is in the heart of God. And scripture tells us..."Eye hath not seen, nor hath ear heard, what God has in store for those who love Him."

We then discover that interwoven into the sentiments written into songs both sacred and romantic, one finds evidence of the correlation between human love and the love of God. It is another evidence of the countless ways God has devised to demonstrate His understanding of the nature of humankind.

God loved us first, and gave us of His breath of life. Still, the interpretation of the word "life" is yet to be fully comprehended. To become sensitive to the limitless depth and breadth of the meaning of the word "love" is to be filled with awe and reverence about all of life in all its forms.

What is this thing called love? It is an element that is compellingly powerful. To know the word is academic. To experience it calls for songs of thanksgiving and praise.

"How do I love thee? Let me count the ways..." Now and then a poet, a writer of romantic songs, or a newly-awakened soul experiences an inspiration to try to count...and gives us a new love song to sing.

Margaret Taylor Gilmore

Proverbs

Monday, May 26, 2000
Proverbs – to Chapter 17:

"Proverbs of Solomon" is written at the beginning of Chapter 10. I am thinking these pages of "wise sayings" are probably the collected gleanings from many occasions when King Solomon was conversing with family, friends, servants or visitors. Possibly some were noted and recorded by scribes taking notes at gatherings and others perhaps, Solomon wrote when he was alone contemplating life, people, and the things that happened that he observed were actions and reactions that marked the ebb and flow of daily life.

At any rate, Proverbs are posted together with no discernable consideration of sequences as to subject matter. They roll along, one after the other, in a way that makes reading them a bit like reading the dictionary. Unless one is looking to find and sort out from the total, thoughts on one particular subject, simply reading the couplets, one after the other, tends to make them all run together and hard to remember any one of them, before the end of the page...

Not only that, but all too frequently we encounter a Proverb stated unequivocally as being a fact, that brings to our minds honest questions and doubts. For example, as is written in Ecclesiastes, righteous people do not always prosper or find fair treatment or safety in this life.

Reading through Proverbs, one finds there a theme of absolutes. Good men are invariably right and rewarded, while evil men are either simple or stupid and they always come to ruin.

But there is great wisdom in these small couplets. They are stated so very clearly and with such certainty, I find among them many that I can easily take to heart for they express irrefutable truths about cause and effect. And some are reassuring and directive.

In total, the Book of Proverbs sounds a distinct call to the reader to "Seek Wisdom." And as I study these chapters, I realize I am seeking wisdom within their content that will enable me to discern more about myself, my life, my world, and also find affirmation of things I hold to be true.

And as I read, I weigh each Proverb in my mind to try to learn more of its deepest truths. Even as I come across the ones that seem obscure, I wonder if I've missed something that is hidden to me at this point. I read to know God's truth more thoroughly so as to know more of how to relate to others...how to be more "wise" in my words and actions. And I long to know more of how to love and be loved, in the way the scriptures say God wants us to love.

May 27, 2000
Proverbs to Chapter 23

All the lines in the Book of Proverbs are thought-provoking. However, though most are perfectly clear, some are puzzling. Now and then, I encounter one I have to think must be a translation error because it makes no sense at all to me.

For example, Chapter 19, Verse 22 reads: "What a man desires is unfailing love; better to be poor than a liar." Standing apart, each line is clear, but putting them together as one statement, to my mind, is totally unrelated content.

But, there are gems of simply stated, but profound truths that sparkle throughout the book. Some statements are repeated so often one can surmise that these are truths gained by way of very personal experiences that affected the very fiber of Solomon's soul. The way he emphasize those basic, fundamental rules for living a good life, that can make one triumphant over adversity, defines a man who desired to be not just a good King, but also a good husband, father, leader and teacher.

Now, as I picture him as a "real person", I have Solomon's own life to consider. Some Proverbs are especially meaningful to me for they express truths I myself have seen proved true. Some I read seem to me to indicate that Solomon was not always certain he had all the answers. For example, Verse 24 of Chapter 20 says this: "A man's steps are directed by the Lord. How then can anyone understand his own way?"

Chapter 21 continues that subject and the two combine in my mind to be one of those unanswerable questions: "All a man's ways seem right to him, but the Lord weighs the heart." And I wonder, "Am I going wrong? What do I think is right, but is wrong?" If Solomon wondered, and I wonder, was that puzzle also one of the questions that inspired the writer of Ecclesiastes to ponder? Obviously most of his life he had tried hard to "follow the rules."

I have thought Solomon was not unlike me, even though he was the wisest of all men, and I certainly am not, we are alike in our sincere longing to be a "perfect lover of God." Nevertheless, life continues to pose problems for me that are like his. Sometimes I ask, "Is that You, God? If You are there, if I'm wrong in this, why did You let me go so wrong?"

When the Lord weighs my heart, He will use scales that are perfectly balanced. I believe this because as I observe nature and know I am a part of all living things, I have a deep awareness that tells me I am forever linked with all life in a place called eternity. And the one who rules that place is the great I AM, whose presence keeps every star, plant, person, grain of sand and every animal, mountain and ocean moving in a rhythm that is balanced and destined to be understood somewhere, sometime...

Solomon's sayings have helped me come closer to finding wisdom through reading his beliefs of how we, being a part of God's creation, should "order our days." He says we are to live simply, thoughtfully, thankfully, truthfully. Always seeking more wisdom to know how to meet each new day with its challenges. What a concept, so simply profound, yet so profoundly simple.

I have been thinking lately of how Psalms and Proverbs express the soul of all of us who "hunger and thirst after righteousness." And how the writer of Ecclesiastes expresses the very same soul of all of us when at the times when everything we ever believed, trusted, hoped for, prayed for seem to be of no help and life makes no sense at all and he says, "all is vanity." It is thought by some that perhaps Ecclesiastes was written by Solomon at such a time in his life.

I find myself in all those books and akin to whomever it was who wrote them. For I have walked through days of bright sunlight and also through dark nights of my soul. When I began to doubt all the things I thought I knew were true and all I had left was a desperate hope that God had not really abandoned me.

That is when I begin to remember Ecclesiastes who finally came to the conclusion that nobody could describe or explain God, but that God is the only explanation there is who could have made all creation...And further, that somewhere there are answers. We just are not yet equipped to understand what it is that He has hidden in our hearts.

I have often said, "I need a really BIG God. I need a God nobody can describe. Unless there is a God who cannot be explained, then there is no meaning or logic, no reason to keep on trying." And, after a while, in time, I have always found a logical reason that makes sense enough for me to return to my "world" and to the foot of the cross.

Thank you, O Heavenly Father, you who are big enough to know my name, along with the names of the writers of those Psalms, Proverbs and Ecclesiastes. Thank you for listening when I pray for wisdom and for protection, direction, forgiving, healing, providing, inspiring, and for divine empowering for each moment of life.

Thank you, O God of God, Very God of Very God, for knowing my name and my soul and the yearnings of my heart. Thank you for becoming more real to those for whom I pray. Thank you for today and for all the tomorrows that are left of my days. I thank You and praise Your holy name. Amen.

Margaret Taylor Gilmore
May 2000

Thoughts on Old Prophets

Reading once again the books of the old prophets, I have come to the conclusion Ezekiel is the mystic. Isaiah is the strongest in the way he makes me "see" more logically why I can know who I am in the sight of The Almighty.

Jeremiah I perceive as a very sensitive individual, a lover of the history of the way God chose His people and led them to the Promised Land because He had promised Abraham He would do so. But Jeremiah's heart ached because he believed God's heart was also breaking because His people had forgotten Him.

Ezekiel was a mystic. From the beginning of his book, we find his relationship with God sounds like a mystery unfolding, but never fully solved. I find his book is mostly about visions that are full of symbolic meanings. And to me, the most powerful part is his description of his vision of what he saw during a guided tour of a temple being constructed.

And the specific point I have discerned that is most clear is that measurements matter. And further...for my purposes as I write, my vision is to try to find how I am measured today in God's eyes.

I began by attempting to review the memories of what I have experienced thus far along my tour of the years of my life. My instinct was to try to find my beginning. When was it I began to clearly remember certain specific moments?

I have written to try to list specific moments I remember, and have wondered why those particular events are the ones, out of countless others, that were the first to come to mind.

Margaret Taylor Gilmore

Isaiah

What a change of tempo! What a dramatic change of subject focus! What a different voice! After the three previous books, Proverbs, Psalms and Song of Solomon, reading the powerful book of Isaiah brings one into a complete and totally different meditative climate.

From the first sentence, a rumbling roar, like the warning sounds of an eminent storm demands our attention. Isaiah's report of his "vision" begins like distant thunder. "Hear, O heavens. Listen, O earth! For the Lord has spoken!" Fearfully immediate, the words are like flashes of sharp lightening, impossible to ignore.

He does not pause. Isaiah puts his words into organized and rapid fire commanding order. He draws irrefutable and awesomely vivid comparisons and makes direct and distinct accusations. His words in that ancient book could be printed today on the front pages of the News and Courier and not be out of date. Currently relevant, we would have to say, if they were put into a news report.

Thus began my reading of Isaiah. After having just finished reading Song of Songs...I found Isaiah strangely reassuring. In spite of his harshness, there is a sense of the underlying "rock" of his faith in a sorrowing, merciful, forgiving, loving God. My thoughts had drifted through those Songs...My thoughts were riveted to Isaiah's recorded vision.

By the time the book reaches the third chapter, the "distant thunder" has already become a very present storm overhead, crashing ominously, full of all the fury of God's pain and sorrow as He observes the pervasive sinfulness of His people.

Isaiah's words must have had impact on some people, for he speaks of "the few who will remain..." In Chapter 3, these reassuring words appear, "Tell the righteous it will be well with them for they will enjoy the fruit of their deeds." I visualize a small bird in a storm, its head under its wing, its feet firmly grasping a tree limb, waiting for the storm to pass.

But Isaiah has chilling words for women who have strayed from worshiping the true God. The condition of women had apparently changed drastically since the early recorded history of those ancient people. No longer powerless chattels, Isaiah observed that women had taken major roles in government...."Youths oppress my people, women rule over them." (Chapter 3, Verse 12) This is a curious statement that would offend today's feminists.

He describes in detail the women he observed who were obsessed with their clothes, hair, perfumes and possessions, manipulative many times in public roles. Not unlike what is being observed in many women today. Could it be that the reason so many people view the Old Testament as being obsolete and "only historical" is because it is so NEW? Ecclesiastes said, "There is nothing new under the sun. Everything that is, has been before."

Considering that extremes follow extremes, one could surmise that after an extreme in the lives of people who have neglected God, an extreme should come to pass that a new extreme could be followed by an old in a new era? Perhaps Isaiah's words are too new, too relevant...to be recognized quite yet by this generation. People, even God-fearing people spend little time reading the old books of the old prophets...

Perhaps we are not yet quite sinful enough for God to put us through the sort of extremes that Isaiah described. Perhaps another Isaiah will come to remind us of what this old book has to say.

But it will come. The gathering clouds and winds and floods will break forth with all God's pent up fury...but there will be a few who will weather it all. Like a bird in a storm, they will cling securely and quietly to a limb on the tree of life.

Margaret Taylor Gilmore
April 15, 1993

Restoring the Broken Gates

He'd heard his grandparents tell how it was before they became slaves. They described to him the "beautiful land", where they had once lived, a place filled with peace and plenty. And they spoke often of the beautiful temple where almost everyone went regularly and joyfully to worship and to celebrate. And the young servant's heart hurt when he heard them weep remembering the end of those pleasant years.

He was one of those young persons people noticed. From the day he entered the palace to serve at the king's table, it was obvious he was different. It was not only his quickness in learning the proper protocol when in the presence of the king, it was his countenance. His face showed sensitivity and he quickly learned to anticipate the king's wishes even before he asked for more wine...

And the king had been noticing the cupbearer, who exhibited an unusual amount of efficiency. As he observed, he began to notice troubled expressions on the young man's face. One day, noticing an especially deep sadness in Nehemiah's countenance, he asked, "I know you are not ill, so why are you looking so sad?"

Nehemiah's explanation touched the heart of the king and thus began the evolving era of the restoration of the beautiful temple Solomon had built in Jerusalem.

It would be a long and dangerous undertaking because the temple had been destroyed, desecrated, and robbed of all its costly decor. Now it was desolate, inhabited only by animals.

Nehemiah was an organizer, a planner and a leader. He surveyed the damage and decided where and how to begin such a formidable task. When he described the plan and issued a call for workers, the tattered tribes responded to Nehemiah's call.

"First we must repair the gates", Nehemiah said. "All those strong gates have been torn down, burned and are no longer protecting the way to the temple." And the sad people's hearts began to hope. Each tribe took responsibility for restoration of one particular gate. And the work began.

America the beautiful is our land. Blessed beyond measure, this country has had trials, suffered and survived wars and disasters of nature, but today this beautiful land is in an even greater kind of peril. The gates that have protected us, those strong moral, ethical and spiritual standards that held us strong for so long have become increasingly and dangerously compromised.

We have tolerated more and more of the erosion of our personal and national moral and ethical integrity. The gates that have protected us are being destroyed, desecrated and denied, and now we are vulnerable to disaster because the gates to the temple are being burned away.

How could restoration begin? Perhaps with words.

Would it be possible that someone with a strong heart will dare rise to lead us in the dangerous task of restoring the gates that should be guarding us from tolerating words that defy all things holy...dishonesty, degrading, irreverent obscenity, vulgarity? Right now, the gate of good words used in public hangs by one weak hinge. What will happen when gentle, pure, innocent, are out of accepted usefulness?

Who may it be in America's troubled heart that will dare to advertise in some Sunday morning newspaper or television promotion that there is a brand of soap, or a motion picture, or a shop selling evening wear or real estate and the ads use words like modest, pure, and/or guaranteed to be exactly as advertised? Who among us will decide to no longer support pornography by attending or buying tickets to plays or music television programs in which everything that is sacred is trivialized? And will resolve to avoid purchasing products that advertise such things?

Each gate needed a team of rebuilders who needed also to always be ready to defend themselves against people who did not agree with what the teams were doing...Today there will be no end of objections, no way to avoid the wrath of people who will not stop threatening the gate keepers. The list of our gates that need restoration are easy to identify. What else is sorely needed are workers willing to face the challenges. But meeting the task is worth the trials it will bring. To whom much has been given, much will be required. America the beautiful fits that description.

Nehemiah was just one man humble enough to ask for help. There may be other "kings" out there, across our land that would be willing to help restore the gates of good words if someone would begin to actually offer to lead the task.

One individual willing to face the dangers of restoring the gate to more reverence for words will find many followers and each one will have picked up one nail at a time in a beginning of the preservation of America's gate of good words.

Margaret Taylor Gilmore

Sinful or Wicked?

Reading the closing verses of Isaiah, Chapter 56, a thought came to me that perhaps there is a difference between being sinful and being wicked.

Isaiah chastises Israel for its sinful life styles, but he follows every accusation with a "but" that assures the people the Lord is always standing ready to forgive. "Peace, peace, to those far and near", says the Lord. "And I will heal them, but the wicked are like the tossing sea, which cannot rest. There is no peace", says my God, "for the wicked."

Then in the next chapter's closing verse, we find the Lord's answer to how a forgiven sinner can keep the peace that passeth understanding. It is to remember to keep the Sabbath Day holy. By keeping that commandment, keeping the other nine will come more easily. Just remembering to obey it will remind us to keep the others. Because when we deliberately decide to focus our attention for awhile on remembering to be thankful for things in our lives that are holy...then the things that could tempt us to ignore Sundays become less likely to cause us to sin.

Might it be that wicked could be a result of a life, or a nation...living weeks and years of endless Mondays? Or like being adrift on a boat without oars, or a fine ship without a captain, lost on a vast restless sea?

Margaret Taylor Gilmore
March 19, 2005

Trust in God

January 8

"Whom the Lord loveth He chasteneth..."

Why does it have to be so hard, God? I try to be "good"...should I not have a right to expect protection?

There is every evidence that hard experiences make stronger people. But that is little comfort when we are in the middle of a heart-rending situation. But it is also evident that to whom much is given, much is required. Trees that survive in unprotected spots send roots deep into the earth to find water and nourishment and they become secure in spite of storms and cold and heat. Old, they stand, gnarled and weather beaten, but ruggedly beautiful, a safe haven for many birds and small creatures, shelters for travelers.

Perhaps when we are feeling lightening-struck, thirsty and bruised...we are being counted worthy to share in Christ's suffering and becoming more like Him. "Trust in God at all times. God is a refuge...and underneath are the everlasting arms."

Store these thoughts in your deepest heart. They will water your roots as you experience the chastening of life.

Margaret Taylor Gilmore

"Islands" by Alice Ward

Who is God?

When Did God Begin?

God of God, very God of very God, begotten, not made, being of one substance with the Father, by whom all things were made...

God was God before all worlds...we confess to believe this as we pray...

Behind BEFORE...where was God? When all those galaxies were being made, did God select one of them to be an earth, and did He then design it, build it, furnish it, green and growing, filled with life? Did He wash it with oceans and rivers and arrange mountains and skies and populate it with creatures and people to enjoy it? Could that have happened, according to God's will, BEFORE the earth we know about began to swirl beneath the hovering attention of the creator of all worlds?

But did that first earth self-destruct from sin and selfishness that caused all the waters to dry up and all the living things on land to burn. And is that first world still out there, dark, dry, and lifeless, one of those silent empty burned out planets?

And did God watch sorrowfully as that first earth passed away, then perhaps, did He not decide to begin again and did He select our earth, a second place on which to place wondrous things? A new created place to be filled with blessings for human kind, and a place where He could send the man whose loving life and early death and resurrection could erase the stains of sin and prove that God is love and there is grace sufficient to rescue anyone who asks Him for help?

Behind, before all worlds, where was God?

Margaret Taylor Gilmore

And Where is God?

Strange thought. When all around there is abundance of evidence of SOMEONE at work. Someone is in charge. Something is out there, and something is in here...inside of us...If that someone, something is anything...a power, a being, natural or supernatural...who can it be...or what...unless it be God? But the question is always...there.

Either everything means something...or everything or nothing, means nothing, or anything. Between these certainties...we dangle. Now and then situations, questions, disasters, heaped up frustrations, lonelinesses, cause us to ask, "and where is God?"

That we should even ask...indicates we recognize the someone, the something. And further indicates the condition that appears to come, inevitably, to those who ask questions, perhaps too hungrily...The condition of the down-spiraling depression sometimes leads to feelings of having been totally abandoned. One believes God is still God...but He has turned His face away, and we are alone, and powerless, without hope and terrified at the thought of dying, without the certainty that God exists for us...knowing us...keeping His eye on us as on the sparrow...

Job experienced the agonies of seeming abandonment. On the cross Jesus said, "My God, why hast thou forsaken me?" The occurrence of spiritual "death" is not unfamiliar to the deeply committed follower. Always we are reassured to learn that after those "nights of the soul" the individual comes forth stronger, with fresh comprehending, deeper, fresher understanding, and with more wisdom about the holy mysteries...and quietly better prepared for life.

And where does all this tie into the subject of the occurrence of sudden joy at the sight of a scarlet leaf in a forest, or a pelican heading home at dusk? Perhaps it is a glimpse of the certainty of the fact that ongoing joy is also a part of God...and all that God is includes joy and peace as well as suffering...Perhaps it is that in the split second return to childhood that happens in our hearts when perchance we see a clump of hollyhocks for the first time in decades, that we experience a foretaste of what will be our ultimate grasp and understanding of time and eternity, and all that is between being born and meeting death.

Perhaps we should educate our instinct to make a written account, reminders, so the reality of those precious moments of blessed reassurance will not be forgotten or lost in the demanding clamor of the circumstances of daily life.

So I will make a rosary, if you will, of my memories of such small things as spontaneous laughter at seeing a young squirrel almost miscalculate the distance between limb and wall, and his graceful recovery of balance and safety, and of the wonderful inner, unspeakable comfort I experience at the moment of the touch of the chalice and the sacramental wine on my lips as I knelt at the altar...And I will bask in the reverence I find in the presence of morning's daybreak, and enjoy the recognition of why I find tears in my eyes at the hearing of music played masterfully.

And where is God? He is the someone, who knows all I do not, cannot know...becomes better, stronger, more secure and I feel a safer knowing...each time I take note of and meditate on and appreciate with inner renewal...the why of those jeweled moments. I have a growing rosary of recognitions that reassures me that we will all be reunited, safe and somewhere...after all the storms and all the darknesses are over...forever...

Margaret T. Gilmore
August 25, 1981

Say "Yes"

Eyesight and hearing and understanding improve with age. Really, at least for me.

For a long time I shushed certain painful memories with, "No, Lord! Please...take that out of my mind!" When hurting, burning, throat-closing memories rose from my consciousness to spoil otherwise placid moments, I prayed, "No!" to God, when dark and forbidding recollections would flood my thoughts and I relived in flashes of pain what I call the Gethsemane times of my life. At such times I would reject the thoughts, flinching as I did, at the taste of bitterness on my tongue.

But one morning it occurred to me that it is always better to say, "Yes" to God than to say, "No." No matter what. I remembered the Bible says, "In all things give thanks." I'm not yet quite able to always sincerely say thanks for all things, but I am learning to accept the fact that in my life's total experiences none are not, cannot, be erased for they are all there. The truth remains, they exist forever as a part of my life's history.

But the greater truth is that God has never failed to stay with me through every Gethsemane. I have lived to smile again, and to learn that beyond the pain there is often bright promise of better things.

I see better now, because I have lived long enough to begin to glimpse a pattern in all life's experiences. I hear better now, because I know how to be quiet and listen to the inner voice that quiets my spirit. I am more serene now, because I have more blessed memories, more sacred memories, than painful ones. I have a memory book in my heart that is an extensive, wide-ranging record of times, and places. ways and faces...and of the beautiful "Yes" times that followed the "No" times. All this helps me celebrate the joy that has overshadowed the intermittent pains that were my small share of Gethsemane.

The pattern of my life's canvas is emerging now, and I like the sight and the sound of what I am beginning to see more clearly, day by day, what God has been doing in my life.

"Wherever I am, God is." I read that somewhere. I knew it all the time, I just didn't really recognize Him. In joy and in sorrow..."Yes"...fits, because God said it first. "That is good" He said, after He had looked at all the strange things in creation that sometimes looked like mistakes, but never were.

Margaret Taylor Gilmore
1969

Everlasting

From everlasting to everlasting, from before eternity began to after eternity ends. That incomprehensible timelessness, and my own time's swiftness from age to age fascinates me.

"My candle burns at both ends, it will not last the night, but oh, my foes and oh, my friends, it gives a lovely light..." Edna St. Vincent Milay may not have been exactly reverent, but she wrote vividly about time and her enjoyment of life.

I, too, like the burning. Somewhere I read: "It is not the candle, nor the wick, but it is the burning that makes the light"...

As the firefly gives light to a summer night...is how I think of my time, my light.

I remember summer evenings, playing in the dark, catching fireflies while grandfather and grandmother sat in rocking chairs on the porch, talking, listening, watching, as I tried to capture light.

I sometimes forget how long ago it was since those nights until I am startled by an unexpected glimpse of myself in a mirror as I hurry past. Instantly my perspective on time is altered, and for a while, my thoughts are shadowed. In my time-consuming life I had forgotten for a while how long it has been since I caught a firefly and put it in a jar to help me see in the dark.

And now, here I am, hurrying to catch a moment to save the schedule of my busy day! The mirror is not kind. The woman is aging, and tired. Should I try to ignore the moment, put it out of my mind and use my strength to its utmost every day? Should I not dwell on the NOW, with all its newness, all its possibilities, all its powerful potentials, and its awful maybes...all of which I am still a part?

Or...should I begin to spend more time giving recognition, honor and appreciation for my yesterdays...and be more attentive to the elements that have blessed my days as I have lived and loved and learned? Should I begin to conserve my remaining physical strengths for leaner, lonelier, uncertain times?

Whatever time is, time is God's instrument. A sense of time should result in a more responsible use of our days and nights. A sense of time should give a format to our existence. Orderliness of how we relate to responsibilities, opportunities, is stewardship of time.

A thousand years is as a day to God. From everlasting to everlasting is like one summer evening. Musing now, as I remember my grandparents watching as I ran to catch a firefly, it makes me think that God is keeping watch over me now...as he kept watch over Grandpa and Grandma, when they were children, catching fireflies in summer nights. I know now that God will keep watch over my children and my children's children in the daylights and in the darknesses of their lives.

We cannot capture fireflies that will light our way forever, but we can look beyond, and see the stars that can speak to us of timelessness and a light that is eternal.

I am still a lighted candle. Time, to me is somewhat like an elusive firefly, circling in the darkness of this age...I am like the candle and the firefly...burning brightly and briefly, twinkling now and then...and always longing to be like the timeless stars...

Now I believe my best, my most beautiful age time will be when it is late and quite dark...then, with my own unique light, ignited by God long ago, now refreshed and burning brightly, I will make my way through the dimness of Time directly and swiftly,...into eternity's morning.

Margaret Taylor Gilmore
In the 1980's

One by One

One by one, face to face, we lead, teach, love, forgive, one by one. "Look into my eyes. I have things to tell you that mere words alone cannot convey..."

From His cross Jesus looked at the thief beside Him, and saw the spirit behind the eyes of the dying man. He heard the plea and saw the truth of how it could be at this point, that the man was able to believe and ask for remembrance, forgiveness, and peace. Jesus saw the real person inside the tortured body and gave the man assurance he was not abandoned nor worthless, after all.

The old professor looked up from his work and into the eyes of the eager, yet insecure young man about to enroll in his class. The student later recalled, "Right away I saw that there were lights on inside of this man, and I said to myself, somebody's home in there....because I could tell he really, really saw me."

The contact was profound. The student stayed and learned not only about Math and Physics and Energy and Space travel. He learned how well a life can be lived, in spite of harsh, unfair things, when an individual knows for sure who Jesus is. That knowing is the taper that lights the candles that glow in the eyes of people who have met the Master, face to face, one by one, and this is the truth.

Margaret Taylor Gilmore
1969

"Girl on the Bridge" by Alice Ward

Contemplation

Holy Mysteries

When we are surrounded by dark, secret terrors, and by public uncertainties that apparently have no solution other than perilous sacrifices that even then may not bring lasting certainty, then we are at last face to face with knowing that only God is left.

When we have exercised our last half-ounce of intellect, experience, education and all our instinctive philosophical and psychological skills and insights and still there is no indication that any or all of these make any difference, then we are at last face to face with our human limitation, and we face the ultimate question of "Why...God?"

That God does KNOW is somehow the certain knowing that gnaws at our brain. But whether He knows and will do something to let us know that He knows...and will do something to show that He cares...is our question. Will our prayers work? Will God listen? Does God see, care, intervene?

When we cannot find any indication that God is going to deliver us from our awful stress and spiritual agony, and long periods of "being strong" and practicing patience are rewarded with need to be even stronger longer...and when, finding there seems to be no light, after all, at the end of our terrible tunnel, then we begin to believe in the power of evil. We do not only begin to believe, but to trust in evil's ultimate success. This is the ultimate triumph of the dark power over our tired spirit.

And, we should never underestimate the fact, the ever-present power of evil, nor the genius of its subtle, devious influence. We are always vulnerable. On guard every moment, though we think we may be, we are always in danger of the gradual effects of the deceits of evil that can erode our ability to know the difference between good and evil in our life's experiences.

Today as I meditated I thought God said to me, "DO NOT UNDERESTIMATE THE POWER OF EVIL, BUT DO NOT UNDERESTIMATE THE GREATER POWER OF GOD!"

We may never understand why illogical, undeserved, unfair, cruel, destructive things happen...and we may not need to understand to survive them. But if we can stretch toward the knowing that miracles of healing, resolution, restoration and peace can come, even in the midst of painful conditions, then we can begin to renew our strength, and we can feel somehow the support of the quiet, everlasting arms, and can sense the stirring of the wings of hope again. If we pray that God's will be done, and can be willing to be made willing when we know we are as yet not quite ready for God's love to work, we may then begin to be able to accept whatever is our circumstance and even able to say thanks to God for whatever the ultimate good is to be made of this...some day.

Then we will have tasted the Grail's true contents, and we will know a little more about holy mysteries, and about the love of God that is beyond human comprehension...as much as the why of our trials is beyond our finite understanding...

Margaret Taylor Gilmore

Deeper Wells I

"Water from deeper wells"...Those words often echo and re-echo in my mind. The phrase has become almost sacred to me.

To me, within those words there is magic and mystery and tantalizing wisps of ideas and of promises of limitless possibilities that invite me to search for deeper truths.

The first time I heard the phrase it was spoken by an individual whom I much admired. It may be that is why those times when I suddenly remember those words, inevitably they come with a sort of certain certainty that it is being spoken by that person.

"Perhaps you are needing water from deeper wells," he said, and pointed to the rows of books on his library walls. And so I read and read and read. At first I assumed that somewhere within those books I would find answers to all my questions.

Then one day it dawned on me that every one of those authors had been just like me...thirsty people searching solutions for life's tests. It was like searching for water from deeper wells. And their writings were to share with other thirsty people the water of fresh truths they had found. And I discovered their writings almost always ended with an indication they had found depths of truths, and a realization that vastly more and greater truths were yet to be found in deeper wells.

Margaret Taylor Gilmore
April 25, 2002

Deeper Wells II

Yesterday dissolved and this morning is beginning to become an elusive element. I cannot hold any moment for very long. "Wait, wait" I want to say, "This moment of springtime is too lovely to let go. I must take time to cherish it."

Yesterday I began to write something about walking in snow in springtime, almost reverently considering the carpet of white dogwood petals that overnight had covered the path at my feet. Then, strangely the phrase, "water from deeper wells" came to my mind.

I wondered why the two thoughts had converged in that context..."I need to contemplate this moment," I thought. Then, conscious of the brevity and the elusive nature of it all, I almost held my breath, waiting inspiration...

Then, from out of somewhere I heard my heart saying..."Wait, wait, these moments contain gems of great truths. They come from a place that is hallowed and holy. You are to hold them forever in memory of one of the times when you have found the way to a well from which you have dipped and are now forever more alive. You have tasted the waters of truth and beauty...from one of God's deepest wells."

"This is the day that the Lord has made, let us rejoice, and be glad in it."

Margaret Taylor Gilmore
April 26, 2002

Dreams and Visions...

Someone said: "If dreams and visions meant something in Biblical times, they still mean something today."

Dreams and visions are mysterious happenings. Some dreams are filled with lovely possibilities, others can be more like nightmares. Some visions become realities, unfolding before our very eyes. With time, all these visions come together to make us who we are.

The mystery is this: What are we to believe about those strange stirrings we feel at certain unexpected moments and how much confidence should we put into achieving those visions, and dreams that may seem like impossibilities? And what about those dreams of finding peace? Or are they visions that glow in the distance like a Holy Grail?

We move toward our future, always influenced by our dreams and visions. They become who we are. As we work though the experiences of the days of our lives, we always remember, at the back of our mind, those dreams and visions we have kept in a secret part of our heart.

And who we are makes a difference to others.

Almost without knowing it, we leave imprints on the lives of the individuals with whom we live, work, play. And we leave something that is lasting and mysterious in the atmosphere of every place where we have lived for a while.

The part of us who dream and see visions is the realist part of us. We are a body in whom a spirit dwells. That spirit is kin to the spirit, and is the part of us from where those dreams and visions appear.

Are you holding fast to your dreams? Your future, even today, is filled with possibilities if you follow those visions, daily asking God to lead you to the place where there is a peace that passeth understanding.

"In all thy ways acknowledge Him, and He will direct your path." (Proverbs 3:6)

Margaret T. Gilmore
August 11, 1999

Suspended

Today I am suspended between realities.
Thoughts frozen momentarily in frames
of wisps of memories float through my thoughts,
signifying seemingly...nothing.
Like vague dreams that have no end.

And I am incomplete, suspended,
without a sense of person, place, promise, or purpose.
But...I think I am...ready for what will emerge next.
I focus on waiting for tomorrow,
for as of now I am drifting toward nowhere.

There is always tomorrow.
And someone is there.
Perhaps tomorrow I will find
I am not suspended. I am
secure, and simply being
made ready for a new
adventure.

Margaret Gilmore

I Wonder

Will I meet Moses when I get to the Promised Land? If heaven is populated with God's chosen people, will that include me? Am I a chosen person? Am I one of those chosen that are descendants from Abraham's lineage?

Perhaps, even from the beginning of their lives some were chosen to be chosen, like Samuel and Isaiah, and some were not...like Cain and Esau? And are some of us destined from birth, to be numbered, like Peter and Paul, among the Redeemed?

Is the New Jerusalem the capitol city for all people? And does it exist for some because they believe it is the ultimate destination for God's chosen and redeemed, and for others it does not, because they believe it is a phantom place, an imagined destination and unreachable?

And I wonder how it happened, and where did Enoch go when he "walked with God and he was not"? And how and why did Phillip suddenly disappear after he had explained the scriptures to the Ethiopian in the chariot?

If heaven is another name for the New Jerusalem, then that is the place I expect to find my grandfather and maybe Moses and Peter some day.

Many years ago I answered "Yes", when Grandfather Taylor asked, "Will you meet me in heaven?", but secretly I was thinking, "I hope so." Now I'm nearer the heaven he believed was to be his final destination, and I still recall clearly his confident statement, reciting the scripture, "I have fought the fight, I have kept the faith, there is therefore laid up for me a crown..."

Now I truly believe when I step over my earthly boundary line, I will see Grandpa and Grandma, and all those generations of the chosen and the redeemed, who have gone on ahead of me to take the place prepared for them since the start of eternity. And if Adam, Abraham and Moses and Isaiah are also there and if they know me and I recognize them...then I won't need to ask God any more questions...ever.

Could it be that heaven is divided into generations, and my generation and that of my parents and grandparents will be together while Moses and his parents and grandparents are in another? Perhaps some are chosen to be chosen before all worlds and some not.

Perhaps I ought not to ask, but how can I deny that I wonder about what comes after this life? Not IF, but where and when and who else?

My Bible reads to me that "broad is the way and narrow is the path and few there be that find it." And..."many are called, but few are chosen." But then...my heart leaps up and I am reassured when I read "My own know my voice and I know theirs..."   And in my innermost eyes I see, and I hear with my heart...and I notice in heaven Grandpa looks to me a little like Moses.

Margaret Taylor Gilmore
May 9, 2001

Perfection

"It was so beautiful it made my heart hurt." I remember hearing that remark made by a college student attempting to describe her feelings at hearing a piano being played with intense sensitivity by a master teacher.

I have experienced what I believe was like what she tried to share with us by that remark. I have felt that indescribable emotion just twice when my own soul resounded to unexpected experiences that surprised me with an exquisite bitter-sweet pain.

I felt as if after a very long time, I was suddenly and unexpectedly reminded and reunited of a time, at a place, or with a person very dear and exceedingly familiar to me. In a way, it was as if I was back in time, or perhaps more as if I was into a future time. Those two moments were far too fleeting to tell which.

Since then I have felt a sort of bitterness because any attempt to describe the experiences to others have been futile. Perhaps I cannot, because such moments are too holy, too so very personal, and far too mystical and mysterious to define in human terms. Even so, I have wished, now and then, to share with someone the shimmering sweetness of the experience.

Sweetly poignant, because I know those mystical moments have changed me forever, and thus I have become somehow more vulnerable to life, and I would like to tell someone it can happen to them...perhaps...someday. And although I remember, I know I can never ever go back to try to discover the reason why those moments seemed so familiar, yet unfamiliar.

On hearing for the first time the words and melody of "Danny Boy" my heart felt as if it had been touched by an electric shock. I found my eyes flooding with tears. I wanted the music to stop. I wanted it to never end.

Entering a great cathedral towering among high mountains, I was totally unprepared for the overwhelming, enveloping sensation of being thrust suddenly into the holy presence of The Almighty. Just as I entered the sanctuary, accompanied by numerous other people who were there to see the famous place, I was all at once all alone, dazed by a sense of profound awe. And I wept for a reason I could not explain.

Some years later I told a good friend what had happened to me in those moments that were crystallized forever in my memory. It was at a moment when I felt here was someone whose wisdom of such things might help me sort out what these experiences meant. This is what he told me, and I think it is the best explanation I can comprehend.

When the inspiration that was the origin of the plan, for the purpose, the place and the preparation materials that made up the elements of such an accomplishment...when all these are brought together through the motivation of the creator of all that is perfect, then something happens to that person who is prepared at that exact moment to hear, to see, to understand. Because...a perfect balance has been achieved at that moment...the person, the time, the place, the purpose of that moment...

I believe that to experience that kind of emotion at that time is to have glimpsed for just a moment, heaven's unspeakable beauty. It can happen in cathedrals, cabins, or in music, paintings, mountain heights, ocean waves, midnight's stars, forests' silent songs interpreted by birds, and in looking into love's eyes alight, in seeing courage, hope and heaven. Heaven is possible, and attainable in those moments when the heart is in mystical, perfect balance with creation and has been made ready to ache with speechless thankfulness.

Margaret Taylor Gilmore
March 18, 1999

Miscellaneous, Personal and Unfinished Thoughts
Nostalgic, Affirmative, Solution and Solace

Slipping into my consciousness...unexpected, illusive, fragmented...are remembrances that now and then rise to the surface of my awareness. Lately it was music that called memories to rise...memories that blessed...and burned...and would not go away.

Perhaps this week it was hearing the Charlotte Choral Society singing. "It is Well with My Soul"...and thinking that is a song I would like to be sung...or played...at my funeral.

Or perhaps it was hearing Lawrence Welk playing songs that for a split second returned me to half-remembered nostalgic moments that I did not know at the time would glow forever in my heart. Those were precious, youthful moments.

(Or were they moments experienced by someone I never knew until many years later. Now I think perhaps it was my true self seeing into the years ahead.)

Or am I? Or was I? Or was it we...you...and...I?

One evening I told God I am willing now to let go... of life's mysteries, memories and dreams, and return to wherever it is that was my origin. To whenever it was that I became a "someone"...and to that somewhere where memories and dreams are not mysterious but can be clearly seen sometime as definitive, God ordained events.

Could we begin again...God...? Somehow...somewhere? Someplace where my memories can be realities...and where my emotions make them a part of the me I am today? I'm just now beginning to see the emerging of a pattern...destiny?

Long ago I heard my father singing World War I songs. I could tell they expressed emotions I could faintly sense but did not understand at the time. I know now he was singing memories. Today sometimes, when I am alone...I sing his songs...they are songs of loving and leaving and longing and dreaming of tomorrows that came, but lasted just long enough to make memories that still blessed and burned. Today his songs are mine. They bring tears to my eyes...for daddy's wistful melodies are now defined in mine.

"With someone like you, a pal good and true, I'd like to leave it all behind and go and find...some place that's known to God all alone. Just a place to we'd call our own. We'd build a little nest, somewhere out in the west, and let the rest of the world go by.".."There's a long, long trail a-winding, into the land of my dreams, where the nightingales are singing and the white moon beams. There's a long, long night of waiting, until my dreams all come true...'til the time when I'll be going, down that long, long trail with you..."

My songs are similar...because somehow...somewhere...something is unfinished for me too. Now when I'm alone, I sing such songs as these: "Now is the hour when we must say good-bye. Soon you'll be sailing, far across the sea"...or "You went away and my heart went with you."

But not forever..."It is well; it is well, with my soul..."

Thanks... for my memories...

Margaret Taylor Gilmore

The Fighting Lady

The wars are over now forever for a "Fighting Lady." Morning and a marvelous sky...A bobwhite's simple serenade and an almost motionless expanse of green, gray and blue invites my attention seaward. I am at peace...in meditation.

In the foreground of my view is the Yorktown, once called "The Fighting Lady", now a museum ship. Its carrier deck holds a half-dozen obsolete airplanes that once were fighters for a war-torn America. Serene now, the ship is set in permanent docking across from the Charleston skyline.

I open my Bible randomly to Revelation. I read of white stones and secret names, and of open doors no one can close and closed doors no one can open...I feel a mood of praise for a long and happy life coming to my mind's focus...and as I meditate...the world comes by...cars begin to cluster at the ticket window and the world's day demands my attention.

Margaret Taylor Gilmore

Stop and Survey the Mess

"Everything is in a mess," he said, speaking from the towering height of his ALL Knowingness. "The government is in a mess. The economy is a mess, Social Security and health care are a mess, and the war is a mess...Everything is in a mess."

Maybe so, I thought. And maybe not. But his words came back to me as I searched through the scattered papers on my desk and strewn across a table nearby.

This place is a mess I thought. I was certain I knew where I had put the paper...in a place where it would be easy to find when I was ready to take care of the matter. But now, one day later, it appeared to have been swallowed up in the "mess" of numerous other papers I had been careful to keep close to my hands.

Methodically I went through everything, again and again. In desperation I emptied the trash basket, then the garbage bag, examining the messy contents, one by one. All the time I knew for certain the paper had not left my house. I was frustrated, impatient and irritated, because it was important that I find the paper, and soon. I was beginning to be a real mess myself.

"Lord," I said, "Help me." Surveying the clutter once again I caught sight of a corner of an envelope I recognized as being important. It was not what I was searching for, but it was something I had forgotten to attend to, and was almost overdue. Thankfully I tucked it under the cushion of my chair and sat upon it.

Next I noticed a folded paper that was a recipe I'd copied and promised to share with a friend. But the real find was a poem, yellow with age, that I'd kept in my phone book for years, because what it says is a reminder that there are some wonderful truths that have not been lost among the years. It suddenly struck me that maybe my mess was a mess that happened so I would find those other papers and be reminded of truths I needed to remember.

Another thought came as I contemplated the interpretation of what is a mess. Sometimes facing a mess means we have to make an even bigger mess in the process of cleaning out, dusting out, discarding out...to clear the clutter away to make room for a distinct orderliness. Some messes require major messes to prepare the way for orderliness to begin.

Someone has said, "Sometimes you have to make dust before you can clear the air." Now I am thinking how thankful I am for the mess that is the reason I have a clean and orderly desk today. If I can find an envelope maybe I should mail a copy of this to that commentator who sees nothing in America that isn't in a mess.

Margaret Taylor Gilmore
November 11, 2004

"The Boys" by Alice Ward

Personalities

A Slave Woman's Story

Night was about to overtake the last of the day's sunlight. I had just finished washing up the dishes when I heard a commotion in the courtyard. The Innkeeper was firmly telling someone that every room was occupied. But then I heard the voice of his wife saying something I could not hear clearly, but it seemed to have changed his mind.

I was ready to go to my own place for the night, but I did not hurry because I was wondering and curious. I watched as in the dusk ahead I saw a man leading a donkey toward the stables. On the donkey sat a woman and I could tell she was in great discomfort. After having known suffering myself, I easily recognized signs of silent suffering. I can tell when I see a hurting person or animal, and I knew this woman was young and that she was in pain.

My dwelling was near the stables, and I paused as I started walking past it. From where I stood I watched a bearded man helping the woman lower herself from the donkey's back. Then he helped her lie down in one of the feeding troughs that were almost full of hay. Impulsively I stepped inside. I spoke to the young woman and told her I would stay as long as she needed me. She said nothing, but she gripped my hand and since that night my life has been very different.

The birth came quickly. I kept thinking how close that little mother had come from having her baby on the side of a dusty road. One learns to be grateful for such things, and I was very glad to have been with this girl woman at the hour when another woman's understanding can be very reassuring.

Then the man fetched a very tightly packed pouch from the donkey's back and brought it to us. In it were garments needed for the baby. My thought was that exceedingly careful preparation for the birth of this child had begun months before.

After I had washed the infant and wrapped him in his drying garments, the three of us began to examine his features and we agreed he was indeed a perfect child. Every part of his body was perfect. His head was perfectly round and his ears were neatly rested against the side of his face. His fingers and toes were long and tampered. All this we admired. Then we took turns each of us stroking his tiny but sturdy feet.

But the part of that experience I will never forget is how amazed I was when the baby first opened and focused his eyes, seemingly seeing everything. I had helped other mothers with their newborns, but I had never seen one with eyes like this. He seemed actually to see into the eyes of the one holding him. First he turned his gaze toward his mother and then toward me.

I was startled because I felt this child already knew my name. There was an agelessness in his eyes that made me feel as if I might be a part of his own timelessness. Since that night I have had a strange peace that does not vanish even when I am in a perilous place. Because since that night I have a peace that is beyond understanding.

Written by Margaret T. Gilmore
November 24, 2004

My prayer – May His gift of peace be yours also and more love to share is my gift to you.

His Name was Noah

He built boats. He built boats to sell. That was how he made money to feed his family. He learned about boats when his father showed him how his boat was built. He learned a boat needed to be strong because sometimes when a day's catch was large and a storm began to make the water rough, his father seemed not afraid because he knew his boat would not sink under the weight or by the waves.

One might say Noah was born on a boat. He could not remember a time when his parents were not talking about building another boat...His mother would shake her head and say, "Always another boat, a bigger boat. I think the one he has is big enough."

And even now, even though he was almost old, boats were as fascinating as they were when he was a boy. In fact, he often dreamed he was building a boat big enough for all his family to live on. "And someday I will," he said to himself.

But he was in no way prepared for what woke him that night. Noah knew immediately the voice was God's. And he trembled, because of what God had said, "Build a boat big enough to hold not just your family, but all your animals too." That was a thought that would take some thinking to get accustomed to build a boat bigger than he had ever imagined building, was something Noah had to think more about...

His first response was to say, "I don't think I can..." But God said, "Do not delay, begin today." God seemed to be in a hurry. That thought was enough to cause Noah to rise from his bed before daybreak. God must be thinking bigger by the day, Noah decided.

The work went more easily than he had imagined it could be. Soon his sons found a forest with enough strong trees to supply wood, and then they discovered they had skills for cutting grooves in planks so they would fit firmly together.

Every day Noah realized his boat was becoming a bigger craft than he had ever imagined he would build. Gradually, and in spite of everything, Noah began to enjoy the challenge. He directed the work, aware that the rainy season was only a few months away.

Neighbors watched with various reactions. Some were envious, some were skeptical. Most believed Noah was more than a little bit crazy. "Spent too much time thinking about big boats", they said wisely..."Like too much wine, too much thinking can make a man lose his common sense."

And there were days when Noah thought they might all be right. He had heard God a second time, and what he heard made him doubt his own hearing..."Make room in the boat for a pair of every kind of creature."

Noah's wife cringed. "Even ants and elephants?" she asked. "Nobody, even you, Noah, could manage that. And even if you could, just think of how bad the whole boat and everyone of us would soon start to smell."

Mrs. Noah wasn't convinced the whole thing wasn't something her husband had imagined. "But he's so certain it was God's voice he heard, and I cannot argue with that."

Noah had to admit he wondered about a lot of things. But he didn't admit that he did. "We will just do what God said," he replied.

After that Noah began to awake in the night and started sketching stalls and shelves, boxes and bowls to fit into the space where the creatures would stay. Some stalls would have to have room enough for animals with long legs and long necks. Others would need to be wide enough to accommodate elephants and strong enough to hold animals prone to be dangerous to creatures smaller than they. And there should be little boxes for bees and little bugs...and hummingbirds.

Finally the big boat was almost finished. Noah watched as his sons poured thick black pitch between the planks and the pitch oozed into small cracks and crevices to make certain the boat would be watertight.

He wondered if God was going to tell him how long he would have to house all those creatures, and how was he to provide food and water for them. Noah wondered and wondered. Then he had a dream, or was it a vision that showed him how to measure with his cupped hands seeds enough, and how much water for every creature, and for his own family.

God had said there would be a great flood that would last forty days and nights. And no creature not aboard the big boat would survive. Noah wondered how the creatures would know when to come to his Big Boat.

So Noah watched the skies and kept on saying, "I think it might rain today." The neighbors were not pleased to hear that, but kept on watching Noah's countenance.

Noah was beginning to be more than a little anxious. And he kept on waiting to hear from God how to coax all those creatures to come to his boat.

One morning a bird outside his window awakened Noah. Right away he knew this bird was different from any he had ever heard singing before. This bird sang so many songs Noah wondered how it was possible. The bird sang as if he might be singing for all kinds of birds. Noah wondered if perhaps the little bird might also be translating an important message to be understood by all the animals. He thought, "There are bigger birds with bigger voices. I wonder why this one is God's choice to carry messages?"

But Noah knew the bird knew the message must be a warning. "Listen, all you creatures, come to the boat. Bring your mate and board the boat, today...NOW."

At that moment Noah heard a solid, steady sound as if an army was marching, coming closer by the minute. Then he saw a great beast of the forest breaking through the tall grasses. And, just behind him was his mate. They headed toward Noah's big boat. Meanwhile, overhead, ominous clouds were gathering and becoming blacker.

"The animals are coming. The animals are coming because they know something is about to happen." Noah shouted to his family. Noah remembered the first time God had said a flood would come and no life will survive outside the big boat. Even then he had wondered, "Not even fish?" but said nothing. Afterward he wondered why he had even thought to ask. If he had known how hard it would be to keep on sailing, getting nowhere for forty days and nights, it wouldn't have mattered.

During those long nights and days...Noah had a lot of time to think about his life before and during the months when he was building a boat that was to hold two of all the whole world's creatures, the more he thought, the more he marveled at God's strange and powerful ways. Noah was tired now, really weary. The ark had rolled and survived the weather, but he longed to see land... somewhere.

The more he thought, the more he knew God was not playing games with His children when He sent the flood that swept all the known world away. God had been hurt and angry because the people He had loved so well had forgotten to thank Him for blessings that had been so abundantly theirs during so many years. Noah was filled with amazement to think God had chosen him to build a boat to protect lives that would help to build another world.

God's heart seems always to be ready to rescue wandering children...even to the point of creating a whole new world when necessary.

Each day he collected rain in big jugs, and he was surprised to find seeds sprouting among spaces in places that astonished him...

And when the rains stopped, it was the bird, the one with a talent to speak in any language, who finally arrived to tell Noah the flood was almost over, that the earth would dry soon and the animals would be free to find places God had already prepared for them to live.

Perhaps the bird that sang in a language understood by all creatures, was the first bird God created to carry winged reassurance and peace to wandering travelers, and perhaps it was really Him, disguised as a DOVE...

God's heart is that big.

Margaret Taylor Gilmore
March 29, 2005

Jesus Loves Me, This I Know

Jesus love me this I know,
For the Bible tells me so.
Little ones to him belong,
They are weak but he is strong

Yes, Jesus loves me,
yes, Jesus loves me,
He will stay close
beside me all the way,
if I love Him
when I die,
He will take me
home on high.

Yes, Jesus loves me,
this I know, for the
Bible tells me so.

Two-year old Sammy sang with all his heart. Now and then gleefully improvising his own version by singing verses out of sequence, or stopping now and then in the middle of a phrase to trip up my effort to match his version as I sang with him. My "error" would bring out shrieks of laughter.

Sammy had been traveling all day, and he was becoming too tired of behaving. He twisted, wiggled and strained against the seat belt, just as we were doing. We were within thirty miles of home when his father suggested he sing a song or two. Soon I was singing, clapping with Sammy, laughing and with as much abandon as he. I was certain the singing was like sandpaper to the nerves of Sammy's father, who had been driving for several hours, but I figured singing was better than spanking, so we sang "Jesus Loves Me" all the way home.

Since that day, I have cherished the memory of a cheerful little boy trying to behave; fitfully trying to obey his father's command to take a nap; resting his head on his father's knee, constantly kept from sleep by sunlight in his eyes...finally finding fresh diversion and endurance for the last miles of a tiring trip by singing that he knew Jesus loves him.

The melody and the words echoed in my mind for several days. I woke mornings with "Jesus Loves Me" running through my thoughts. Sometimes, in the middle of the night, I would wake and hear those words and that melody...gradually I began actually listening...really considering what those simple words meant to me.

Then, visiting a friend in a distant state I experienced another strangely emotional encounter with that song I had learned in Sunday School when I was a preschool child. My good friend Elaine plays her grand piano with skill and with real sensitivity. On a remembered occasion, she improvised, weaving hymns together as one uninterrupted melody.

Slowly, gently, softly, she began a one-fingered rendition of "Jesus loves me, this I know, for the Bible tells me so." Gradually, without pausing, she began a more complicated, yet still exceedingly simple weaving of other songs into her music. "The Old Rugged Cross", "How Great Thou Art", "Wonderful Words of Life", "Be Not Dismayed, God will Take Care of You", "It is Well with My Soul", "Abide with Me", on and on. Gradually, she played with more intensity, more volume, finally, with triumphant fervor, "The Hallelujah Chorus."

Then gradually Elaine softened the music of the continuing series of melodies, bringing the series, without interruption, back once again, softly, slowly, gently, to her one-fingered, confident, "Jesus loves me, this I know, for the Bible tells me so."

Remembering, even at this moment, the "almost too wonderful to bear" emotion I feel when she plays, I am moved to tears of a mystical joy. At last, I have discovered that "Jesus loves me, this I know, for the Bible tells me so", is profound power appropriate to be the theme song of individuals of any age.

Little Sammy has learned the truth of that song because he is young enough to believe without question what it says, because his parents have taught him it is true. Thankfully, I have learned the truth of its message because I have lived long enough to have seen it proved in my life and in that of many others. Now I too, believe that "Jesus loves me, He will stay close beside me all the way, if I love Him when I die, He will take me home on high."

Margaret Taylor Gilmore
June 30, 1988

How God Answers Prayers

He is eleven years old. He is a student in a church denomination school. He has complained a lot about "all that stuff we have to learn to say." He has said he wishes he didn't have to go to that kind of school.

The family of parents and two children planned a trip to Florida for the holidays. They loaded everybody, including two dogs and a cat into the family van and were half-way to their destination when something went wrong with the car. The repair was being done at a station at the edge of town and it was taking longer than they'd expected.

As they waited, it was a good idea to let the dogs out of their cages, and with leashes well in hand, were allowed to run about. The area was on a busy highway, and across from a wooded area. The younger of the dogs was eager to run and twisted his head from the collar of his leash. He ran toward the highway, then back toward the wooded area. Various people attempted to catch him, but he playfully eluded everyone, dashing back and forth from the woods to the highway.

Meanwhile, the boy was crying, sobbing...saying, "He'll be killed. He'll get hit by a car..." His mother told him to sit and hold tight to the leash of the other dog, assuring him somebody would catch his dog.

Finally the dog did exactly what they didn't expect him to do. He turned and dashed straight to where the boy was sitting, who quickly caught the dog between his legs and held on while his parents reattached the collar and leash.

At that moment, the boy looked up through tear-stained eyes and said, "Mom, it's true, prayer really does work."

And that event made this year's Christmas an especially blessed one for the whole family. After visiting grandparents, the family returned to Summerville, and Eric's parents are thankful that Eric knows for sure now that God really does answer prayers.

Margaret Taylor Gilmore
January 18, 2005

Golden Harvests

Afterward, all of us wondered why we'd been invited to her home for a wonderful dinner that evening. The hostess was an elderly lady I had met only once or twice before. We were members of the staff of writers, reporters and "Ads" people who worked on the city newspapers. None of us were well acquainted with her.

The memory of that lady and that evening has continued to tug at my heart. The conversation around the table seemed not very spontaneous, even though we tried to find a beginning comment or question that could spark a flame that would lead to a common ground of shared mutual interest or experience. The evening left me with a lingering impression of something unfinished or unfulfilled.

Afterward one of us remarked, "I think she doesn't know she is old." I've remembered that too, and the idea made me feel we had somehow made her feel even older than she was, because the evening was not exactly a success for any of us. Something was missing. We had not "connected" with our hostess.

Now I know she knew very well that she was "elderly" and that she looked old. Today I know it was her heart that was not old. And I believe it was her ageless heart and her agile mind that had planned an evening with people who might share some of their Now-ness with her. That lady had lived long enough to have experienced most of the essences of being a woman in a fast changing world. I believe she had lived a full life, loved, lost, traveled and most of all I got the impression she was one who knew who she was, and who she would always be.

Now I know she knew she was old, but hoped to have a conversation in which the differences in our ages would not matter. I know now how she must have been eager to engage in conversation with people whom she thought would be interested in sharing tales. Perhaps personal, or perhaps descriptions of individuals who were being written about because they had done interesting things. She believed people who were writing about people to whom the adventure of being alive is always a current event...would be delightful in dinner companions. We missed her cues.

Old. Was it because we unconsciously assumed there was an invisible uncrossable space called years between us? We were all at the "high tides" of our years, she was experiencing ebb tides and nearing the beginning of the low. That night the tides of our lives were washing up on the different shores.

Some years later I wrote a piece to which I gave the title, "The Golden Harvest." It was the account of an interview I had done with a lady who was a resident of a retirement village. It was her one-hundredth birthday. I asked her to tell me something about her life when she was a young woman, and how she felt about her life as it was that day.

I spent two hours with her, and heard a fascinating story. She had lived a hundred years, and had accumulated a harvest of experiences and an amazing amount of wit and wisdom. And besides all that, she was still young at heart.

"You know so much about so many things," I said. She replied, "Honey, if I don't know some things now, I haven't been awake all these years."

I had noticed she was wearing a pretty bracelet, and I mentioned that I admired it. She hesitated, smiled shyly, and confessed it was a birthday gift, "From a gentleman who lives down the hall."

Since that afternoon, my own birthdays have climbed to numbers that proved I too, am chronologically "old." And now I think I have an explanation of the reason that dinner party was not exactly what any of us had anticipated, and why our hostess must have felt sad as she cleared her table of the china and crystal and silver that were symbols of the years she loved to remember and had secretly hoped someone might ask her to talk about.

We didn't ask because we were too young to think about a time when "old" would become a personal word. Gradually the effects of age had diminished the self confidence our hostess once possessed. And she was not bold enough to offer to speak of her life before she was old. But for us, in the climate of insisting demands of our Now-ness, we were absorbed in matters of the moment and not aware we were in the presence of someone who could have given us glimpses of a life that had been lived abundantly and as adventuresome as ours. And find it as fascinatingly familiar, and later perhaps even prophetic.

I've thought how fortunate I was to glimpse, in that conversation with the "birthday lady", how enriching harvest of gold, can be discovered simply by pausing to ask an "older person" for a comment. Or a story to compare, or by asking a question that may be answered by a voice spoken from long years of experience.

So it happens gradually or by someone's calling us elderly...that we all discover we are destined to the fact that growing older is required of every one of us.

To become aware sometimes, that we are harvesting experiences that make us who and what we are to the people with whom we live...to be able to sort out from the weeds those grains that are God...these are the harvests we can remember, evaluate and sometimes share with others. The best harvests are treasured when they are shared to make memories that will be remembered by others because they are proof that life is an adventure, a journey worth the risks.

So how does it happen, why does it come as a surprise most times, and how does one learn to live with the fact that growing old is a requirement if we live past adolescence?

Margaret Taylor Gilmore

Hal's Question

He was new to our area. I wasn't entirely sure he would fit into the rather irregular systems required for a worker to be effective in my office.

But there was something about him, something in his face that tugged at my attention. It was his eyes. I could not get away from an impression they held the look of a hurt animal. He was quite tall, very thin, his hair thick, slightly curly and needed cutting. And his complexion was scarred. The Director asked if I would consider "taking him on" as a student assistant...I started to say I'd think about it. But my heart twisted with a feeling I still cannot quite define, and I heard myself saying I would take him.

The next day we went through the routines together, and I explained that probably no two days would be the same. Most would be uneventful and he would find a lot of tedious hours doing boring things with old manuscripts, letters and office correspondence.

It was evident from the start that he was very bright. He surprised me at how quickly he understood the convoluted systems of my office. After an hour of showing him about I said, "Now let's talk." I asked him about his family, about his life before he came to us. And I asked him if he attends church.

"Not regularly," he replied, "I like to go to different churches to see how different ones do different things." I asked if he had a Bible, and he said he had "some pages out of an old one." I had a paper bound Testament in my desk and gave it to him.

Then I asked if he believes in God. And he replied that he did. And then we began working together. Three days later as he was preparing to check out for the day he stopped by my desk and asked if I minded if he asked me a question.

"Not at all," I said. "What do you want to know?"

I shall never forget the question he asked. I had never heard of anyone who had posed that kind of question. Certainly I had never thought to ask such a question. And his face and his question have stayed close to the front of my mind ever since.

"Do you think it is alright if I feel sorry for God?" He was perfectly serious. I thought a minute then asked him why he was sorry for God.

"Because," he replied, "God made the world so beautiful, and gave people so many wonderful things, and people are always doing such awful things to one another."

I told him my Bible tells me God created us in his own image and if that is so, then I can think God's feelings can be hurt, just the same way ours can be hurt, by our not appreciating the daily blessings God gives us, and by our being mean, cruel, and doing dishonest things to each other and to nature. His question is one I often ask because I think I too am often feeling sorry for God.

Margaret Taylor Gilmore

Garden Awakening

She looked like springtime, her face alight, her eyes sparkling and her step brisk as she came up the walk toward my door.

"I've been putting my flower garden to bed," she announced. "That's what I do in November. At first it makes me a little sad, but when there is no color, not one left of all the blossoms, and all the stems are dried and drab, then I get busy. I clear the ground as completely as I can of all the dead stuff."

"I try to pat the ground smooth, then scatter pine straw over what may be roots that will sprout next spring. Then I feel good about my garden again."

Below the pine straw her garden is sleeping. Soon the ground will be cold, dark and still as death. In the winter days ahead my friend will look from her window at her sleeping garden and she will imagine what kind of seeds and baby plants she will plant when she has removed the pine straw that has been the blanket protecting the places where some seeds and twigs are sleeping.

Our gardens are silent now, but in just a few weeks people will begin to remind each other how many tomorrows and how many weeks will become months until a day will dawn when garden lovers will remove the blanket of straw and announce to the garden that it is time to rise and prepare to be ready to smile once again into the face of a sunny springtime.

I believe a vision of a tomorrow when she will be working in a newly awakened garden is the reason why my friend was walking with spring in her step and why it seemed to me that morning was in her eyes.

Margaret Taylor Gilmore
November 9, 2004

November in the Rain

She was standing on a street corner and at her feet was a small collection of items that appeared to be odds and ends of the sort one keeps for a while, then usually tosses into a waste basket.

The weather was miserable. It was late November and drizzling rain. My first impression was that she was cold, and the next, that she was selling her belongings for what she hoped would be enough...

"She's out of work. The rent is overdue, and she's scared", were my thoughts as I came near her. I paused to glance at the pitiful assortment and noticed what appeared to be a rolled up calendar. I knew I needed to buy something.

"May I see that?" I asked. She showed me a color print, long, narrow and undamaged. It was an open sea scene, a blue gray ocean churning its white-tipped waves beneath a gray and gold evening sky. And above, between the waters and the skies there were white winged birds in flight, arranged in graceful formation. It was one of those scenes that make one think of the phrase, "It's the going home time of day."

When I asked the price, the girl hesitated and for a moment, then I gave her the two dollars she asked for. I had a fleeting impression she really didn't want to sell the print. I wanted to ask why she was there, selling those things. But she seemed unwilling to be drawn into a conversation, so I took the rolled up print and went home.

I have thought of that event many times, and it has always reminded me of a poem someone read aloud to us at church years ago. The text of the poem was as if Jesus was seen standing huddled against a building. Rain was falling, it was getting dark and the crowds were hurrying to get home. The poem related Jesus asked for nothing, just stood, cold and shivering. No one seemed to notice, or to care. The final line goes something like this: "And Jesus, cold and alone, remembered Calvary."

I have thought of the girl-woman waiting on the street for someone to buy her belongings. Her modest sign said, "For Sale." She was not ready to sell her body, but she was offering all the treasures she had left simply to get through another day.

The print is framed and I look at it almost every day. I treasure it more than other framed scenes that are far more costly. The memory of that girl, that day, still haunts me. Whoever it was who responded with paint brush to the mood of the sea that day, painted himself/herself into the canvas. I believe the artist's response to his view of the sea must have translated something that touched the heart of that girl and it touched something in me the moment I saw it. What the something did was to connect the three of us, drawing us together, in our memories forever. Of things such as these are life's mysteries made.

And I've thought many times...that young woman was once somebody's baby girl. Somebody loved her, someone cared, I have wished I could go back in time to that cold November day...and if she's there on the corner, I'll ask if she will let me help her find a warm place to stay, and I'll tell her I care and I'll be her friend if she needs me.

Margaret Taylor Gilmore
November 8, 2003

Gardens Can Grow Forever

"Peonies are blooming in our garden!" The remark started a conversation around the luncheon table and it led into a sort of Mother's Day epic told by one who is living in Summerville and restoring one of those fine old homes.

We asked what other flowers are blooming there and she told us that in addition to the usual azaleas and Lady Bankshire Roses, there are numerous other kinds and colors...and as she described it, we could sense that to her family theirs is a garden of living memories.

Perhaps it was providential, and perhaps it was near to Mother's Day, because as we listened to her story we were touched, somehow reassured and thankful.

"Our garden is a special place to our family," our friend said. And she described how special are the flowers that are blooming this springtime in her South Carolina garden.

Tall stemmed, colorful and stately, she described the garden's flowers that are springing from roots of flowers that once bloomed in her mother's garden in a state far distant from South Carolina. As she drew out the threads of her memories, she led our thoughts along the path that brought her flower garden to bloom this springtime in Summerville.

When her mother died several years ago on a cold February day, this mother's child wept knowing it was the end of a wonderful era of her life. Now having become a mother herself, she measured the years and the love, and she remembered the flowers that bloomed each spring time in the garden her mother had loved so well.

After the funeral, as she stood gazing from a window at the frozen patch of ground that had been her mother's flower garden, her heart ached, for she knew this was the end of a time and connection to a place where her heart had been anchored during her girlhood years.

Her husband stood watching as she looked toward her mother's garden and he saw them as her tears began to flow again. Then a sudden impulse took root in his thoughts. Without explanation, he took his coat and went out the door. The temperature was freezing cold and the ground was hard as rock. But with an axe and with his determined blows, a large pile of frozen earth was accumulated. And embedded in the lumps of soil, there were frozen roots, bulbs and bits of smaller and unidentified roots of other plants. Which root, which bulb, which was flower and which might be weed, he could not tell. But the big box of "dirt" went to South Carolina with the family.

Wherever they moved and had ground, the chunks of soil went with them. Planted and replanted, those sturdy chunks of dug-up dirt, every spring those roots, bulbs and whatever else, always yielded a storehouse of flowering plants.

Since then after more than a dozen years, the family has moved to their second home. And always the box of roots and bulbs have been dug up, and during some periods they have been sheltered in a place that is safe until they can be planted in another garden home.

This week, our friend told us those roots have continued to thrive and produce generous flowers. And this year, some are blooming just in time for Mother's Day. As she remembered and mused, telling the story of her mother's garden, and of her husband's tenderness of heart, she smiled and there was a gentleness in the room that made us stop and remember our own gardens and our own mothers. She smiled, and so did we because it seemed to some of us that it was a sort of sacred story.

Our friend has given us a new tale we can tell each other and our children's children, because hearing her, made us feel reassured in our own locations and we are newly aware as to how amazingly well roots that matter can withstand being bitterly cold, and/or being moved far from home and still survive to live abundantly, anywhere they are loved. Mothers know about such things. That is why people often remember Mothers' Day with gifts of flowers.

Margaret Taylor Gilmore
April 24, 2004

Glimpses of Glory

He described an event of many years ago when the family was returning from a long trip. It was night and the three brothers in the back seat had grown tired of nothing to count or people to watch in cars that passed beside them. In their boredom, they had taken to elbowing each other in the ribs and shifting their feet to move a foot beside them further and further away. Short bursts of complaints and accusations were interspersed with asking their father, "Are we almost home? How much farther?" To which the replay was, "Ask me that one more time and I'll let you out to walk home the rest of the way."

The one in the middle gave his brother a sharp nudge in the ribs and as the one nudged told the story later, "I was thinking I'd like to kill him for that." He clenched his fists tightly, ready to aim for a blow, when suddenly the car's headlights revealed a road sign that everyone recognized as being very near the turn off to the way home.

Telling the story, my friend said, "When I saw that sign, I unclenched my fist, because suddenly I didn't want to kill my brother." He added, "It was as if everyone had caught a glimpse of glory."

That is one of the stories among others that have become favorites to share when journeys seem to become longer and longer, and tough situations seem never to show signs of getting any better.

I have seen glimpses of glory myself, experiences such as when an impossible situation became possible in one single moment, by way of one simple act of kindness, or was mysteriously and instantly solved, and the only way I could find to explain it was because a fervent prayer had been answered.

On a cold January morning, I was leaving church and paused to contemplate the lovely old church and the pastor standing to shake hands with the exiting worshipers. Then as I was musing the morning's peacefulness, I looked upward beyond the tall buildings to admire the cloudless, sapphire blue sky, sparkling in the morning sunlight. I paused, and deliberately took in a deep breath that chilled my body from the top of my head to the end of my toes.

And what I felt at that moment was that something wonderful had happened...not only to my body, but in my spirit. I had an impression that my entire body had been purified by that stinging coldness. I felt I had experienced God's breath in a way I had not felt Him quite so physically before. It was similar to the sensation I experience when I feel the sting of the wine on my lips as I kneel in communion.

And I thought, "At this rare moment of total awareness I have experienced a glimpse of glory. I have seen the glorious sky and I have tasted God's gift of cleansing air. I am ready now for the rest of my journey, because I have glimpsed another of God's signs by the wayside. It tells me I'm not far from home."

Margaret Taylor Gilmore
January 18, 2005

One Shining Moment

He knew he was good at his job. He knew the boss had chosen him for this job because he knew that Tom knew, and the boss knew a man who knows and knows that he knows is a man who can be counted on to come through when it really counts on doing the job right.

He knew he could maneuver those powerful, massive cranes to touch down exactly where they needed to go. Tom was ready, but he was also aware this job was one with no margin for even one small readjustment along the way. The job had to be done perfectly the first time, no matter what the weather, the time of day or his own personal state of mind.

The object to be placed aboard a ship was a highly guarded secret, one of a kind. And at this particular point was one of the most critically needed weapons of the Big War. Much was riding on his special skill to move that container safely to an exact spot aboard the ship waiting to transport it across the ocean and beyond.

When he told me the story, he was well into his eighties. As he described the memory of that day his countenance changed and his face seemed to became less aged...his eyes brightened and his entire body straightened as if to come to attention. It was as if he was reliving those moments that had demanded the best of all his mental, physical and spiritual gifts.

I could almost see the young man sitting at the controls of a powerful machine, ready to take on a challenge that was more than a test of physical coordination. It was a task that would be a part of a battle in which potentially lay the destiny of countless people. His skill and his standing within his community of fellow workers, all were becoming a willing sacrifice, a tremendous wager. The results would make a difference for the rest of his life. Somewhere in his mind, Tom sensed he was about to take the biggest challenge of his lifetime.

Tom was not a particularly praying person, but watching his face as he spoke I got the distinct impression that as he began to move the crane into position high above and toward the box of precious equipment, that his heart was asking the Lord to keep his eyes and his hands and his mind in perfect balance as he slowly, cautiously edged the crane into position.

Eye and hand coordination converged, and in his thoughts there was a conversation as if he was talking to himself. "Don't think, just do it. Get it right. Just do it right." He reached out, grasped the gears and felt the weight of the lift of the fork as it hovered over the box. "Easy, easy, don't move too soon...easy, easy...", and he began to feel sweat under his arm pits and wondered why he was not aware of anything other than getting the crane's jaws exactly into position. "Down, down, easy, easy, don't close them quite yet...mustn't fasten them too soon...make certain they are right THERE...must make certain I don't close the jaws too soon...must make certain they are tight, right there...before we lift..."

Below, watching from ground level, the word "we" was a part of similar silent self-conversations within the thoughts of other workers. They may not have known exactly what was in the box, but they knew it was a moment that mattered to everyone, because they knew Tom had been chosen because he was the best in the business for precision loading. It was as if every man's heart was beating with Tom's. All eyes followed the movement of the crane.

And then the box, now suspended above the ship, was ready to be positioned over the exact spot where it would stay until it would be off-loaded at its destination.

At that point, as he related the incident to me, Tom's voice quivered with the remembrance of those final breathless moments. It was obvious he was reliving the most significant moment of his lifetime. For on that day, during those moments when his heart stood still, Tom experienced a powerful knowing that made a difference for the rest of his life.

As the mysteriously important box settled safely exactly on the spot aboard the ship on which it was to travel, Tom felt relief, release, and he relaxed thankfully.

It was as if now he knew there was a reason for his being who he was and where he was, doing what he did. He became aware there was a powerful reason for his being alive that day. It was a time of new believing. Not only in his own personal skills, but in the Being he had sensed had been with him as he gave his whole body, mind and spirit into doing what he later realized he had been born to do.

It was years later as he reflected and retold the story, that he began to be so deeply moved...again...at the memory of how powerfully he had been guided on that day.

"I was just trying to do my job." He said, as he finished his story. When he leaned back in his chair, it was then that I saw a distinct smile brightening Tom's rugged countenance. I caught a glimpse of how it can feel, growing older, and to be warmed by memories of shining moments.

Margaret Taylor Gilmore
February 20, 2004

How the Skinny, Mangy, Nobody's Dog got Lucky

He was born like any other puppy, filled with energy, ready to learn, ready to play, ready for the big world. He was a wiggling bundle of happy potential. He was the kind of little creature that could cause most any child to squeal with pleasure when a puppy would lick his cheek.

But life had been difficult for this puppy. He had grown up to expect rejections and abuse. He had not had a child to play with or to laugh when he licked his hand, or to help him chase a ball across a field.

The workers who were building a house had seen the dog, skeleton thin, mangy, flea-bitten, starved, and slinking around the place. They had tried to ignore him, assuming he would wander away.

But that day when the "boss" came by to check on the progress of the house being built for him...one among several others...he happened to notice the trembling, fear-filled starving dog. The sight troubled him, and when he was preparing to leave the site, he made a quick decision. He loaded the dog in his truck and took him to the office of a nearby veterinarian.

"Take care of him," he told them. "Do whatever you can for him...I'll be back to get him..." He left two-hundred dollars and said he would pick up the dog after they had done what they could to make him less miserable.

The big, soft-hearted man was exceedingly busy and wondered how he was going to deal with the situation he'd gotten himself into. He called his father, asking if he would take care of the dog until he could decide what to do about him. He was thinking he would have to turn the matter over to people who help animals...whoever and whatever they could do.

After three days, the "boss man" called his Dad and said, "I'm going by the Vet's this afternoon to pick up the dog I told you about. I'll have to turn him over to somebody who can decide what to do...Would you and Mom be willing to take care of him until I can find where to take him?"

And so it was that the unwanted dog was going to have a temporary home for a day or two. Nobody really could figure out what exactly could be done...until the day the "boss man" called his Dad and said, "I'll be by in about an hour to get the dog. I've got to take him somewhere..."

The response was, "Nope, Son, we aren't going to let you take this dog to some place where they may decide to destroy him. Your mother and I have been so touched by this dog's gentleness. Besides that, we can tell he's smart. We've already named him Lucky, so you just don't worry about coming over to get him. He's our dog now."

And that is how Lucky came to be a member of a family where there are grandchildren and great-grandchildren who think he is the best dog they ever met. Now Lucky is healthy, his coat is shiny and his tail wags all the time. Not only that, he can lick a child's cheek and help chase a ball almost any time a child comes to visit his family.

Margaret Taylor Gilmore
January 13, 2004

"Shadow Memory" by Alice Ward

It's About Time

Is that You, Lord?

How can I know for sure the voice that talks to me at times, from somewhere deep within my consciousness, is a voice from God? I have prayed faithfully for guidance, direction, solution, protection, and I have heard what I thought was God's voice and felt what I thought was His presence. Can I be sure it is not simply my own "want-to" echoing?

What do I do about my self-questionings, my doubts, my wanting proof? I am learning that sometimes it is in retrospect as life unfolds that I can see proof...evidence in episodes that in sequence, show clearly that indeed the paraclete is always beside me and messages are God-sent.

Other times, I am assured and reassured through tangible confirmations. For example, I have been awed when after concentrated prayer for guidance; I have opened my Bible to find a passage standing out boldly, almost as though there were no other words on the entire page. Words that lock in to exactly the answer the questioning my prayers have asked. These are profound and moving experiences.

Now I know that I know...that I can trust the voice within, for it is a conversation confirmed through experience and through scripture and illuminated by a light so defining that now I can go...unafraid into life's light or darkness, listening and attentive to the voice within...

Margaret Taylor Gilmore

Say Yes, God

The preacher told us about his dog. She loves to run with him. At daybreak each day, they take to the streets and run together. Greeting the morning along with the squirrels and the unfolding flowers, they run beside the water, pacing their steps to the splashing sounds of the tide as the waters strike the sea wall. Together the tall, muscular man with the smiling eyes and his big black Labrador, greet each new day with shared joy.

Except now and then, when the preacher has commitments that require he leave very early, too early to allow time for the usual running-with-his-dog time. He described those days: "I'd sit drinking coffee and my dog, with her head on my knee, kept looking at me with those pleading eyes, asking why we aren't running. It tears at my heartstrings. I try to explain it isn't that I don't love her and it isn't that we will never run again, and tomorrow we'll be out again on our regular routine.

"I keep talking to her, but she never seems to understand. One day I thought, perhaps this is the way God feels when we pray and pray to Him for something He cannot let us have...at least not just at this time. He keeps trying to let us know that just because our prayer isn't answered "yes" right now, it doesn't mean He doesn't love us, He has other things that have to be fitted into our lives first."

Why not today, Lord?

Because, perhaps, tomorrow will be a better time. "Trust me", the preacher tells his Labrador. Now I hear God's voice saying to me, "Wait, tarry, the solution will come...I will answer, I will come..."

Margaret Taylor Gilmore
1969

How Did It Happen? Why?

I read it, impulsively copied it on a piece of scrap paper, and kept it, folded into a small square in a corner of my wallet, forgotten for awhile. Months later I found those words I'd notice, hand lettered and framed, in the den of a friend's home. He didn't know who wrote it, or where it came from. He'd simply seen it, copied it and found comfort in it. Since then, these words by an unknown someone, have "spoken" to me many times.

> "The Lord may not have planned that this (unexpected traumatic event) should overtake me, but now that it has, though it were an attack of an enemy, by the time it reached me, it had the Lord's permission, and all is well. Because He will take it and make it work together for my ultimate good among all my life's experiences."

The thought is easier to accept perhaps when life is going smoothly, but when disaster strikes it helps to have a positive thought to share. The phrase points to scriptures that encourage me..."Rejoicing in hope, patient in tribulation, continuing instant in prayer..."

Later: I have a feeling that whomever it was who wrote the sentence about God's intervening for our ultimate good into anything that can happen was probably written by someone who was desperately casting about in search of a "reason" to explain a personal Job-like catastrophe.

And So...

I'm still musing. Life is filled with unexpectedness...with predictability and with mystery. From everlasting to everlasting, from before eternity began to after eternity ends...is an incomprehensible timelessness...and my own lifetime's swiftness of passage is obviously a part of it all. The marvelous and the mystical, the uniqueness of each individual and our inescapable relationship is with everything... and with everyone...past, present, future...

The concept fascinates me. "My candle burns at both ends, it will not last the night, but oh, my foes and oh, my friends, it gives a lovely light." Edna St. Vincent Millay may not have been exactly reverent about the way she looked at life, and at time, but she spoke vividly. I relate to her analogy.

I, too, have learned to like the burning. "It is not the candle, nor the wick, but it is the burning that makes the light." As the firefly gives light in a summer night...I identify....As the candle that is ME burns steadily...Dear God, let me glow with a lovely light...

My thoughts are tempered today with a curious combination of a sense of being balanced between a yesterday of a long, long time ago and a tomorrow that is yet far in the distance, yet closer than today.

I remember summer evenings, playing in the dark, catching fireflies. My grandparents sitting on the porch talking, listening, watching as I tried to capture lightening bugs.

I often forget how long ago that was until now and then I am startled by an unexpected glimpse of myself in a mirror as I hurry past. Instantly my perspective on time is altered. I had forgotten how long it has been since I caught a firefly to put into a jar to help me see in the dark.

And here I am, hurrying to catch a moment to save the schedule of my busy day. The mirror is not kind. The woman is aging and tired. The wax, the wick and I...burned away...by Time.

I cannot ignore that it is I, nor that I have lived through many Mondays, Fridays and Januarys. Should I try to put it out of my mind and use my strength to its utmost every day? And is it possible that I learn to ignore the mirror's image and dwell on the now, with all its newness, all its possibilities, all its powerful potentials...its awful maybes...the NOW that perhaps I can still be an actual, active, meaningful part of?

(And, please, God, if you will indulge my vanity, would you let me be yet, for a little while, a little lovely, too?)

Or...should I begin to spend more time giving honor and appreciation to my yesterdays, and remembering gratefully those dear hearts and gentle people with whom I've lived...and learned...and loved...? Some now lost...gone on ahead and some...like me...waiting...to see...more of me?

Should I try to forget that growing older isn't what I'd thought I'd be doing so soon...And begin to dwell on dawns that come after peaceful sleep and sunlight that comes after rains? And thus conserve the strength of the time that is still mine? And perhaps quietly discover among the hours of each day, new ways to share what time and life have taught me?

Whatever it is...time is God's instrument, God's gift. Our most precious possession...Whatever it is, time is indefinable...brief and eternal.

From everlasting to everlasting is like one summer evening. To those who love to think in terms of timelessness, the thought is reassuring. To others it presents a terrifying prospect...It is said..."A thousand years is but a day to God..." What day is today...for me, God?

As I muse, gratefully remembering Grandpa watching as I ran to catch a firefly, I know God is keeping watch over me, just as he kept watch over Grandpa, when he was a child, pursuing fireflies in the evenings of his boyhood.. I am reassured that God will keep watch over my children and their children's children in all the daylights and the darknesses of their lives.

I am a lighted candle. I am a firefly. I've been captured by the love of the great creator of all light...My best experience...my most beautiful, triumphant time...will be when my path on earth darkens, and with my light, kindled and ignited by God, I find my way through the dimness of time as I now know it, into eternity's morning.

Margaret Taylor Gilmore
Written Over Time

Thoughts on Time, Mystery and Silence

Someone has said: "Life is not a test we must pass; life is a mystery to be solved." Ecclesiastes says: "There is a time for everything...and everything is beautiful...in its own time"

Among these thoughts, if we sort them out, are clues to the holy mystery that is life. Most of us find it difficult to achieve a balance between believing and having faith in the concept of God's beautiful timing...and the often painful and pressing demands of our complex lives.

Ecclesiastes gives us one clue to the mystery..."Eternity is in our heart, but we do not recognize it." Inferred is the thought that perfect timing and solution to all our questions is in eternity. If indeed, eternity and heaven are already in our heart...that thought brings increased awareness of the sacredness of each hour of our life, we will "spend" our time more carefully.

If we can practice reminding ourselves that life is not a test we must pass, then we can begin to think of each day as a part of a mysterious journey toward a heavenly destination. We will find that gradually we begin to recognize clues as to who we are and who God is, and with that discernment, how to conduct our lives with greater confidence.

"In quietness and confidence shall thy strength be." This clue is vital. Because it is in silence, solitude and prayerful meditation that we become most able to clearly hear mystery's calming, reassuring voice.

Margaret T. Gilmore
January 1995

Elizabeth O'Connor, author of *"Search for Silence"*, has written:

> "Prayerful surrender to God from the core of one's being brings about a fundamental change in the quality of life, so that life comes to be lived on an entirely different level of existence.

> "...Mysterious as this may sound, it actually has to do with changes in very ordinary aspects of living, such as increased awareness of what we see and hear, a heightened degree of receptivity, a growing capacity to respond, to be engaged in the moment as one who is fully present.

> "...Surrendering to the quiet inner wisdom of the mysterious bedrock presence of the Holy Spirit within one's life and personality...the calling of every Christian."

Almost There

It happens at unexpected moments...alone, or in a great hall, listening to great music...sometimes...I believe I am ALMOST THERE. Over the horizon, beyond the here...And it seems as if I am about to know...When those moments arrive, I believe if I can climb just a little higher, dig a little deeper, concentrate a little harder, or walk just a bit further upward, I will know. If I can, then perhaps I will know more, or much, much more than I know now.

Is it the presence of the most high God that I feel in the silent solitudes that echo in my soul? Is the creator of all worlds the one I think I have heard...in those moments when I am being caught up by the "lift" of the music of the spheres?

Is it the heavenly music, captured for a while by the instrumental mastery of an inspired symphony that my soul becomes once more an elemental thing? And when I am swept above and beyond the explainable, definable here...am I then nearly to the crest of the place of knowing?

But the moment passes, and I am left with a vague impression that I have almost grasped a new and very great awareness. Now I believe that someday, someway, I will KNOW. And that will be the moment I will see the place I have come to and know the one that I am. Then I think, the angels will sing and God will smile.

Margaret Taylor Gilmore
September 1, 1998

Memories

I remember...yellow roses, blooming on a fence beside a country road. I remember...being a first-grader, en route home after school, struggling to wade through waist-high snow, then being lifted into the strong arms of a neighbor who, through his window, had been watching his own children alight from the bus, and had observed my difficulty as I trudged toward my home. That was the year when several children, trapped in a stranded school bus, froze to death.

I recall being amazed the next morning to see my grandfather digging through snow that had drifted to above the double doors of the barn, and discovered beneath it a white goat, still alive, standing against the door.

I remember being surprised when I was called out of class to be told I had been chosen to play the "lead" role in our school's annual Christmas play. I think I was in the second grade.

I remember the musty smell of a "dug out" cellar, combined with the odor of bags filled with apples and potatoes. I remember finding far back in the dry cold recesses of that cellar a china jar, turquoise color, with a hunting scene on the front...wrapped in old newspapers...its origin still a mystery.

I remember many perilous climbs on a barely supported ladder to reach the "loft" of the barn where I often went to look through old books that had been stored there since before the 1920s. Now I believe they were school books for advanced students in business and science. Fascinated, their strange content kept me going back to look again, but I never knew exactly what they were about or to whom they had belonged.

I remember a gray cat Grandpa Taylor named Samantha. She was born without a voice, and her "meows" were silent. Mornings she would perch on a gate post from which she would leap to ride on Grandpa's shoulders to the barn where she would be given "squirts" of milk, aimed into her waiting open mouth from the udder of the cows being milked.

I remember storms, rain, snow, hail, and one that had to have been a tornado that left a small twig from a tree imbedded straight in, like a long nail driven, into the frame of a kitchen window.

And dust storms...We soon learned the early warning signal. Mornings when the western skies were clouded with a dusky rose hue, we knew another dust storm would soon blow into our valley. Some days the dust was so thick it totally blotted out the sunlight, and we lighted lamps at noon to see. My desk in study hall was beside a window, and days when the dust was finest and thickest, even though the windows were all tightly closed, I could write just one line at a time and before I could write the next, it was necessary to pick up the paper to shake it free from a film of dust.

I remember certain teachers. Mrs. Etta Stilwell, my first Sunday School teacher, mentor, neighbor, was an example to me in more ways than I recognized until years after she died.

My fifth grade teacher, Mrs. Alice Houston, who encouraged me to become "a writer", which set the course of my life's career. I remember Mrs. Effie Koons in high school, who would not allow me to do less than my best. In her I found an example of "tough love". And "Miss Lucille Stubbs", who found in me the same potential as did Mrs. Houston, and saw to it that college was to be my destination.

I remember Bert Powell, who was seated beside me the night our class graduated from high school. Sitting there, it suddenly struck me that this hour would be our last as a class, to share the same room. There I was, dressed in a long white dress, holding a long-stemmed red rose. "Hold Fast to Your Dreams", the speaker was saying...At that moment I became distinctly aware I was about to pass a milestone in my life. I felt tears, not knowing for certain why.

Afterward, Bert and other "fellows" with whom I had never before had more than a passing conversation, seeing my tears, came to me, expressing genuinely sensitive, comforting, appreciative words. I think I was not the only one who became aware that night that not only would we probably never see some of us again, but that life, as of that night, had taken on a totally new definition.

The year was 1938, and World War II was about to change many of the things we never dreamed could be changed. Bert was the first member of our class to die in that war. Delmar Zeiger survived the worst march of the war's events.

Within two years my life was drastically different. I remember feeling adrift. Since my grandmother had died, my grandfather was sharing our home with his daughter and her husband. Somehow, after that, I felt our house was not my home, even though I was welcome there. I needed an anchor. Even if I had known I needed a counselor, I had no one nearby to whom I could look for advice. I married because it seemed the logical thing to do. I went into the union an innocent as to exactly what the act might mean, or require of me in the future.

I remember the miracle of motherhood. From the day he was conceived, I was aware this child would make a difference. While he was being born, God sent a vision into my sub-consciousness, and I wondered what it meant. Now I know and I am amazed because it became a source of reassurance.

I remember the "war years." I remember hearing a seemingly unending drone of planes flying over our house near Mare Island's Naval Base. Later I learned Japanese submarines had been spotted, cruising along the California Coast.

I remember VJ Day and the celebrations. I remember my son and I going to the grocery store, followed by "Skippy", the little black and white dog I had rescued when he was an abused pup. Skippy, waiting outside, had not seen us leave the store. Tad and I could not join the Victory Parade until we found Skippy. I remember feeling guilty because my joy was overshadowed by a "lost dog", but we were soon reunited and together as we entered the throngs in San Francisco celebrating the end of World War II.

Margaret Taylor Gilmore
Unfinished June 29, 1999

Timepieces

When clocks and watches needed winding to enable them to help us keep track of days and hours, it seems to me that time was gentler, quieter, friendlier. Now our clocks and watches do not need winding to keep on ticking, they depend on batteries to give them life. We have lost, I think, a valuable partnership. We miss participation in the accounting, the checking with an authority...and no longer needing to check the accuracy...we have lost a subtle opportunity for a reminding awareness of how and what we are doing with moments, weeks, months, years. We have relinquished our part of what clocks and watches are meant to do. Most of us no longer wind timepieces and most of us would rather not be reminded of the passing of time. But time keeps on winding its way through our lives.

Time seems noisy now, too loud, too demanding. We've lost the awe at the idea of time that was symbolized for many of us by the friendly movement of a pendulum measuring the hours. Too often now the hours seem to push us rudely, without regard to how overwhelmed we feel, and how out of sync our swift-passing days appear to be.

I liked those old clocks that ticked and struck. I liked the gentle, rhythmic reminders of minutes that were passing. I like the memory of the sound of a key winding the spring back to life. I miss hearing the reassuring, "bong, bong, bong" of the telling of the hours. The clock's steady sounds were something to depend upon, whether the house was full of people or we were one alone. In those days, the clock needed us, and we needed its reliable companionship.

Once, long ago, a citizen of a small town told me, "Each time the clock in the tower strikes, I ask myself, what have I done for God in the hour that has passed since I heard it strike the hour before?" The memory of that remark, like the clock in the tower, has never stopped reminding me of the significance of every hour of my life.

I've always had a sense that time is my friend. The sounds of our old clock on my grandparent's mantle, ticking the minutes away, signaling the hour to go to bed and the hour to rise, or the hour to gather around the table for meals, those sounds bought our family together. Now and then, over the years, sometimes at a late, late hour in the night as I woke from a dream or lay worried and apprehensive, the clock's quiet, regular ticking was always reassuring. Some part of me felt safer, knowing the clock and I were together, and in time, there would be another day.

The timekeeper of my life has kept a faithful account for many years. Each night my physical "spring" is renewed by sleep time, and each morning my spirit is refreshed, nurtured by the presence. When the clock of my life has run its full span, and is ready to mark the last hour of the last day of the years of my life, I pray it will strike a reassuring, comforting, and accurate sound in the night. I will have no need for a key to rewind the spring, for time will have accurately measured and completed the number of the moments, minutes, days, weeks and years of my life. Thanks be to my time's keeper for the adventures, the abundances, the answered prayers, and for the love that would not let me go.

"Time has laid his hand on her heart. Not striking it, but as a musician places his hand gently on the instrument to quiet the quivering spring..."

Margaret Taylor Gilmore
Written November 24, 1992

It is Sunday Again

I am thinking of the fragileness of time, the delicacy of days, and the preciousness of moments...They do not last. Sunday mornings, especially, I am aware of love and loveliness and how recently it was Sunday...last Sunday. The thought of time and Sunday-feelings...delights...and frightens me...because...I'd like to hold them both.

There is no lastingness, no forever, here on earth. No Sunday mornings I can keep, no year that will withstand the calendar's turns, not even one small moment I can hold, even for a little longer. All of time sifts through my fingers and all that remains is memory. All that lasts is spirit. All that continues to move, and have meaning, throughout time...is spirit-talk between God and me.

God and me...we are the WORD. The WORD is in the perfume of springtime, and in the chilly darkness of winter. Life's springtime. Life's winter. The word is in the idealistic passions of youth, and the realistic decisions of maturity...those paths taken after much prayer and sleepless nights...The word is a friend's hand, stretched forth in understanding, a symphony, a shout of joy. The word is a birdsong, a love song, a meeting and a saying goodbye forever, a sacrifice, a gift received.

The word surrounds me and calls me upward and onward.

What God has said to me and I said to God I have written from the real depths of me, and I have kept because my journal of conversations with God is tangible evidence that we were together...all those days...Spirit to Spirit.

The word remains, because God defined it, and I wrote it, as I heard God say it in my heart.

I am, God IS, WE ARE...together and this is a blessed, holy mystery...The spirit is timeless. Being a spirit-child, I, too, am timeless.

Margaret Taylor Gilmore

Autumn Time

Thanks I give, for time to think
about autumn time...and us.

Thanks I give for fresh, fall winds,
cool against my face.
Landscapes royal, rich,
sapphire skies, birds in flight,
tireless seas, smoky, misted mornings,
velvet nights, mountain tops.

Thanks I give that I may watch
a world in change, and know somehow,
that change is good, when it comes in time.
And thanks I give for faith that knows
some things never change,
and become more precious with time.

Thanks I give that I am not alone.
I am part of a holy mystery that is a blessed fellowship,
born of truth and faith that creates a unity of love
that encircles time, place and space and embraces
all those people, places, spaces, and all those autumns,
springs, summertimes, and wintertimes that I have ever loved.

I am thankful because I know that holy truths
are from everlasting to everlasting, and do not ever change.
Except at the seasons when I am changed and gain more
understanding, and a larger, greater truth appears. Then I
can be more thankful because I know I am becoming more a
part of endless, holy mysteries. Because of this, because of You,
I am comforted. I am reassured. I am grateful. For
this I know...along with love's vast worlds of galaxies,
oceans, seas and lands, creatures majestic, and creatures
small, I too, am known.

Margaret Taylor Gilmore

November Contemplation

November is here. Quietly now, I think I must go aside and apart from the environments that crowd my thoughts. I always forget that November is always like this. November means the pace of life quickens, my heart tightens, tension mounts. I need to remember...

Lord, as I try to catch up with my calendar, let me not overlook small miracles that happen and the spoken and unspoken prayers that are answered along my hurried way. Help me to believe there really is time enough for all I really need to do.

Amid all these questions and pressures, let me hear thy voice, and in the answers let me know for sure that it is You. Let me not miss the messages that your angels are still bringing. Even today...the message is Your personal message to me...for today. Help me to remember...in noisy November, the quietness of the soul, the serenity available, for those who take time know enough to remember that all of time is yours.

Today...I am strengthened as I remember...relationships that are no longer a part of my everyday life. Let me remember the wit, wisdom, courage and examples I have known in the lives of departed ones whose immortality is assured because of my recollections of the richness of our kinships. They come to vivid reality as I remember...lasting kinships of our spirits.

Forged by God's design, memories of family relationships that helped me become aware of a divine creator...and friendships, those precious relationships that have been mine that come flooding to my thoughts...The recollection of those individuals is poignant with the perfume that transcends distance, death and decades of time. Precious shining moments, and years of mutual support are relived in my thoughts, and prove the pure quality of trust...these are everlasting covenants of love.

Weekend Again...

Monday. Again. Mixed emotions about time. How could time have simply evaporated? Friday was only yesterday...except...much has happened since I wrote Friday at the top of the page in my journal book. More emotions, more movement...than two days should have held...An unexpected visitor, a report of a death, a letter, a call, a trip to a distant destination...a surprise, all made a difference. None had been on my calendar of events. My heart hasn't had a weekend of rest. Tomorrow is Monday. Monday is just before another Friday. But I'd rather wear out than rust out, any time, Grandma said.

June's Here...

Overnight my calendar says June 5 and I hadn't finished May! I read somewhere a theory that perhaps time does not pass...that we move through eternity and we make our own time's way through the experiences we call years.

I don't know what difference it would make if we knew for sure whether time...or we...move through eternity. We are children when we begin to be aware of the mysterious element called time. When we are children, it appears to us that years are very long. During those years, most of us are impatient to arrive at the age when we can take charge of "everything." Then gradually we become aware that to try to get a grasp on time, and take charge of everything, is as difficult as attempting to harness the wind.

At the autumn time of life it is easier to believe we are the moving parts...that time stands still and we move through it. Along the way, we have encountered life's adventures and experiences that made us who we are when we are old. "Too soon old, too late smart," we say.

And at autumn, whether we are young or old, time seems to accelerate. The more familiar we become with life, the way weeks, months, years come and go...our times become like a road traveled daily. The distance between Januarys gradually seems to become shorter because the months are all so familiar. The smooth, the rough, the bright, the drear...by the time we have lived to mid-way...the road of life has become very familiar.

We begin, after a while, to realize that where we walk is the road toward home...We know because the path is becoming more recognizable...Finally, we find the road is leading inexorably toward a mystically reassuring destination...and soon, for some of us, getting there quickly becomes a secret desire difficult to explain to people younger than ourselves.

We do not need a map. We have by now learned that "My tomorrows are all known to thee...I will follow, follow..."

Margaret Taylor Gilmore
Sometime - 1995

A Meditation before the Year 2000

I'm told that for most of us, we think of time as being a circle with "forgiveness." If we don't finish something today, we think, "If I can't finish this today, I can finish it tomorrow. If not, I will have this week. Even if I don't finish in a week, next month will roll around and I will have time then to get this accomplished."

But at the approach of a New Year, we tend to think of something completed, or something we believe is a lost cause. Time has finished twelve months. We think of the final days of the year as if it has reached the end of a straight line. One circle of twelve months of tomorrow's opportunities in increments of days has come full circle. The year is done. It is a finished work.

We think of the New Year as being another beginning, another opportunity, a challenge to meet whatever comes with cautious hope. At twelve o'clock midnight there is for most people a brief moment, before the clock strikes, that is filled with mystery and magic, awe and anticipation, and the memory of countless generations who have lived through the length of their days and years surviving somehow triumphantly because of the timeless, reassuring light of the faith, hope and love that seems to forever hover over all the earth.

In these few, short days before time becomes once again a straight line ahead of us, perhaps even this new century can be anticipated with joy, by thinking about it is as if we are about to set out on a journey. A journey of months on a never before traveled highway of time's path, soon, ahead of us there will be a new path, a highway of days, a journey of weeks and months. Along our way there will be signposts and crossroads requiring decisions, and challenging paths that invite us toward experiences, adventures, dangers, pleasures, opportunities, responsibilities.

We can meet each day of the circle of the months with expectant gladness, saying, "This is the day the Lord has made. Let us be glad and rejoice in it." Thus we will be able to live expectantly, moving with time toward the light that shines, even in the darkest unknowns, prepared to meet each day with thanksgiving and prepared to meet danger and even death with courage.

Then, at the end of the year 2000, we will wonder why sometimes we wondered if God was still watching, listening, and in charge of His creation. The path of each year is always straight. It is a journey that leads toward completion. The light that brightens the circles of the sometimes gloomy days, weeks, months along the way is a star.

Margaret Taylor Gilmore
December 6, 1999

A Tale to Take into the New Year

She's the kind of person who refuses to try to prevent squirrels from taking refuge in her attic. She says they come when the weather is cold and so far, she's found no evidence of wires being chewed or other damage. She laughs about the way they roll around up there, sounding as if they are playing with bowling balls.

On the afternoon of Christmas Eve, she was driving down a Charleston street and saw a tiny bird fluttering in a puddle. She turned her car around and went back to rescue it. By that time, the family who live in the house in front of the puddle had started to drive away, then they too had seen the bird. They too have a heart for God's little creatures.

It was a team effort. Everyone helped. My friend took the bird to her home and started calling veterinarians. She was told of a new vet in Mt. Pleasant who specializes in taking care of injured birds. She drove across the bridge and found the office. It was Christmas Eve.

The "bird doctor" examined what they believe is a Wren and found the bird had suffered a broken wing. He told my friend he would take care of its wing and would let the bird go free as soon as it has healed.

And that is a Christmas Eve story. It has all the elements of a Biblical parable, and when she told me about it, I felt blessed, just hearing the tone of joy in her voice, filled with thanksgiving. And it was New Year's Day when I decided it is a tale that needs to be told...I am reminded of the song..."His eye is on the sparrow, and I know He cares for me...too."

Margaret Taylor Gilmore
January 3, 2005

Who's Listening?

"Listen and the world will hear you."

These are the words that are woven into the pattern of a colorful silk scarf, a gift from a friend several years ago. I had not noticed the sentence until after my friend had left, nor did she ever explain what she may have believed the message meant. Perhaps it is part of something written into a poem or a book. Perhaps I will find it somewhere, sometime.

I have wished I could find the origin because it continues to this very day to test my imagination. I have thought this; the someone who wrote this sentence was attempting to express an idea that he/she believed was worth sharing. And the thought was how much the world's people needed to learn about each other. In some circumstance, the idea caught the attention of an artist who designed the words to be included in an intricate design for a square of pure silk. An inspiration, perhaps, because he found in the words translation for an inner sought solution he was needing to hear.

Still, like pieces of an unsolved puzzle, the words cling firmly to the innermost parts of my mind. The sentence has a haunting quality, like a call from a distant place. I wonder if it is a code, a secret message from a past wisdom, or a cryptic message of a future significance, emerging ahead of its time. Whatever it may be, I share my thoughts this way...

So...today I share someone's thought message that is expressed in what seems to be in a language I am unable to translate. I wonder, is it a warning, or is it a promise? Perhaps it is both, according to how each person interprets it.

And now I am reminded of another sentence I remember from some place, I've forgotten where..."Life is not a test we have to pass, life is a mystery we keep trying to solve." Put the two ideas side by side and somehow they seem to connect. And from deep within my soul, I hear an echo of yet another sentence that is unforgettable..."In quietness and in confidence shall thy strength be."

This I know because it is from experience. There is much to learn from time spent in silent solitude, listening with confidence to hear the voice within. In times of testing or in times of thankfulness, I have learned that the voice will fill my cup with reassurance, because I have waited, listening.

And I know that solution to all of life's mysteries are never solved because new mysteries, new tests are always out there with every tomorrow, bringing another day, month, another year for us to meet and attempt to meet triumphantly. It is well to remember that it is in moments we spend in quiet confidence that we pass the tests that help us solve mysteries.

And there are times when confiding in others the test that we have experienced may become opportunities to translate for struggling others, the solutions that can come from investing serious segments of their time in quiet solitude, thus to gain confidence in the act of listening.

And then our own words and ways can become a translation of the clear message that is our confidence in the one whose voice the world is waiting to hear.

Margaret Taylor Gilmore
August 7, 2004

Larks and Harps

"Time," he said, "Has laid his hand on her heart. Not striking it, but gently, as a harpist lays his hands upon the strings to quiet their quivering."

And the memory of her lingers on, as from the heights we can hear the distant notes of a lark's sweet song. She was our friend, gone now, but we are not sad, for from afar I think I catch the scent of lilacs that she loved, and from the heights I think I can hear a melody that is a lark's song.

I think the distance may not be too far between us because even from the heights, I think somehow, between our today and our yesterdays, we will find our way to where she is. And we will know her by the scent of the lilacs that she loved, and we will recognize her voice, pure and sweet, like that of a lark that was like her life...for she was always seeking newer heights from which she could glimpse her tomorrows.

Today we think of her that way and are comforted that now she has heard the lark's sweetest songs. And I think she waits with eagerness when we will hear it too.

On a someday all our harp strings will be stilled until another time when they will quiver again, remembering. And then the fragrances and the sounds of the earth will be ours to enjoy once again.

Then everyone who has ever been stirred in our soul by such things as the scent of flowers and the songs of birds, will rejoice, remembering each other...And the strings of our harps will quiver with joy because all who have ever known and worshiped the creator and have loved one another will be together again on the highest mountains where lilacs bloom and larks rest, now and then, between songs...

Margaret Taylor Gilmore
April 22, 2004

A Lesson in Black

I bought it for just a few cents. I found it on a shelf in a dusty little shop that was going out of business. It was a saucer-shaped cup atop a graceful pedestal. Intricate etchings marked the brass, reminding me of the sounds of bells on a camel's harness, and the sight of rich colors woven into silk carpets.

The pedestal dish had been stained by the apparent spilling of a substance that had spread and blotted out the delicate markings over much of the cup. And no one had wished to buy a spoiled thing, even though it was a lovely shape, and offered for a very small price.

I do not know why I could not resist it, except I was drawn by the thought that the person who had created this object, etched it, polished it, must have been entertaining beautiful thoughts as he worked. "Love has gone into this object's making," I thought.

At home I brought out a variety of cleaners and used a generous amount of diligence, but the stain remained the same. After awhile I put the pedestal aside, and once more the lovely creation was rejected. But I could never bring myself to throw it away, and some twenty years later I came across the pedestal and wondered why I had kept it so long. I decided to try, just one more time, to remove the disfiguring stain. I applied fresh brass cleaner, and I rubbed and rubbed. Nothing happened, except the unstained parts gleamed beautifully. As I rinsed off the cleaning chemical one last time, I thought I saw a place where it seemed to me was a lessening of the blackness. I wasn't sure, but my resolve increased. I applied more cleaner and rubbed harder and with more determination than ever.

Then, through the swirls of paste, I could tell I was making a tiny bit of progress. For more than another hour, I scrubbed and rubbed and polished, and when I finished the entire pedestal and cup gleamed and not one trace of stain marred its beauty.

I love my brass pedestal dish. It rewards me every time I look at it. We are linked by love. We've defeated ugly. We've overcome rejection. It took time, patience and hard work, and it took believing in believing.

Now what the pedestal's creator dreamed is true once again. It is useful...beautiful....The lesson here, I think, is...through Christ...I too am overcoming all dark things that once stained my bright spirit.

Margaret Taylor Gilmor

Two Worlds

The older my body, the smaller my "outside" world has become. Hearing, eyesight, physical strength diminishes and restricts the wide-ranging activities so taken for granted in earlier years. My role on stage is now just a "bit part", a walk-on, now and then. The spotlight seldom shines on me. And that is jut as well for I am realizing my skill as a "public performer" is no longer what it once was. For many years, I was a full participant in conversations, in career, church and community activities and in family matters.

Now, gradually, I find I no longer long to take part in activities, because the field is no longer level for me. I am no longer a part of a generation in charge. Technology, theology and social orders have shifted...changed...evolved...and I have paused.

I am beginning to realize that with the shrinking of my outer world, there is a gradual enlarging of my "inner world." My focus is keener in the way things I see connect with things I remember having heard, read or experienced. I now sense I am part of a larger space, a territory I find more interesting, more enlightening, more exciting than the world until lately, had absorbed my attention.

I have discovered of late that those experiences, events, emotions, and individuals who absorbed my attention in former years have become the elements out of which the grand mosaic of my life is made. They are not lost. They are still with me. Together they compose a mirror, a prism, a crystal ball, a background, an interpretive view for me...revealing a vastness of awesomeness and glory...A world not visible to me until very recently.

Thoughtfully, prayerfully...I contemplate who I will be, whom I will meet, who will also remember the world that was...ours...when in my next world...I find myself newly born.

Margaret Taylor Gilmore
1995

"Good Morning" by Alice Ward

Mornings

Morning! Morning! Morning...Good Morning!

Just that one word stirs us. Willing or unwilling, morning is ours to deal with. Ready or not the word makes us know we must be ready for it. Something about the sound of it strikes into our deepest awareness. Morning is a powerful word. It demands our attention.

A bird, awakening in the cold pre-dawn, offers a sort of testing, and sings a two-note song - just once... Then he waits, and does not sing again until another creature makes a small awaking sound that alerts another bird to answer sleepily.

I am reminded of a story about a child who learned to play the piano...a five-note melody, with just one finger. There wasn't a lot of it, but he loved the music he could make, and would try out any piano he found along his way.

One day his mother took him to hear a famous pianist. They arrived early and the child strayed from his mother and made his way to the grand piano. Hesitatingly he touched the keys and played his little one-fingered melody...He played the notes once, twice. Then he felt a large presence standing behind him, and a hand reaching across his shoulder.

"Don't stop, keep on playing," the man said, as he placed his hand over that of the child. Then an amazing thing happened. The master pianist played notes that fitted between and into the melody of the child's one-fingered five notes song. And together they made music of a very special kind. The people were astonished and delighted because the music they made was beautiful.

The touch of the master's hand and the child's willingness to play all that he knew how to play, resulted in a concert that touched the hearts of everyone who observed the evolving scene. The people who were there to listen never forgot how the one-fingered melody played by a child, became a masterpiece.

And there is the story of Thanatopsis, a young rooster in a barnyard who was born knowing exactly what would be his life's special assignment. He was supposed to wake early every morning, just at sunrise, then it was his responsibility to announce to the world that morning had arrived.

So he began his career one day at dawn when he tried out his announcement voice for the first time. So he crowed with all his might, "Morning! Morning, Morning!" In the big house people who had been sleeping soundly were startled suddenly awake by Thanatopis' shrill young voice. "What on earth was that?" they asked. But then it wasn't long until they were up and beginning their day. When asked why he was moments ahead of sunrise when he began to crow, Thanatopis explained, "I thought if I didn't start crowing early it might never be morning." Thanatopis was eager to practice his talent and begin his responsibility...

One gentle word, one willing hand, a one-note melody, one act of kindness, of thanksgiving, of gratitude can be powerful. A morning that begins with grateful remembrance that this is another day the Lord has made, and now is a time to be glad that it has begun...is one very good way to greet one another with saying, "GOOD MORNING!"

Margaret Taylor Gilmore
June 2004

Misty Morning

A thick fog shrouded the morning. The mist, almost rain, was caressing my face. And even the stillness was a softness that seemed tender to the touch. I sensed I was experiencing something that was rare and perfect. It was like an interlude between reality and fantasy.

So clean, so pure, everything was exactly right...and everything was waiting. I, too, was waiting, but not ready to relinquish the mood that had taken my thoughts away from time, and the mist had moved any memory of other times and places out and away...if they had ever been there, they had vanished into the mists.

I was drawn to the softness and the silence. I wanted to be part of it. I wanted to be enfolded in the experience. I was seduced by the idea of becoming lost forever in the mood of those moments.

Then I began to be aware that something was missing here. I brought my thoughts to dwell on the question of what was missing. I began to listen.

Then I knew it was bird voices I missed. Birds do not sing when a fog is dense. Birds do not leave shelter when God places His hand on the wind and silences even the whisper of clouds moving to hide the morning sun.

It was the presence of the Almighty that lowered the fog and blanketed me with a mist that had muffled the sounds of nature. Now I could barely make out the outline of a tree nearby. Transfixed, I almost held my breath...reluctant to release the pure and silent softness of what I had felt.

At that moment I heard a swift flutter of wings, and from a few feet from where I stood, a bird swept past, almost at eye level. Then he landed on a limb just above my head and began to call his mate, and from across the garden she replied. My mystical moment was past, but my heart is still thankful... remembering.

Margaret Taylor Gilmore
January 11, 2005

A Morning Psalm

In the quiet of the pre-dawn day I stand outside my door. I cup my hands and say aloud, "Thank you, Lord, for this new day"...and I lift my heart in gratitude for the night of protection and rest that has restored my body from its weariness of yesterday.

I listen...perhaps to hear a creature stirring, a bird awakening, or a vagrant breeze to stir the leaves on the giant old Oak tree. The silence is soft, and I notice a light glowing in a small upstairs window of a home nearby.

I'm imagining that this new morning and I have the world all to ourselves. "It's just you and me, Lord," I say. And my heart composes a psalm of thanksgiving.

"In quietness and in confidence shall thy strength be." Those words come to my mind as I begin the routines that are familiar to my every morning. While I make coffee I look out of the west window to see if there is a glow about the trees that will mean the sun is rising in the east.

I begin to read the "next chapter" of the Bible. I write in my journal about those Old Testament individuals who lived in those perilous times. And I wonder about those kings, plain people, prophets and priests...I write my questions to God asking why, if when, how and what am I to learn as I read prayerfully to find fresh wisdom and understanding.

Next I write the prayers of praise and petition I made for myself, and then I write a prayer that those same prayers will extend to cover all the people for whom my heart reaches out to touch with love.

Soon I begin to hear morning sounds from the street. I turn on the kitchen radio to learn the weather forecast. The cat has come in and the telephone is ringing. For a little while morning had been God's and mine alone, but now the entire day is mine in which to live...and share...with the world.

Margaret Taylor Gilmore
September 3, 2004

Seeing the Glory

Mine eyes have seen the glory of the Lord. He is springing out His glory into every blade and blossom, and into every lovely corner of the garden where I live. And I have heard His voice inspiring me to prayerful worship, and grateful praise.

Sheltered there amid the glory, I stood musing and looking upward...morning was new and as my rested spirit paused, I contemplated the protective canopy of leaves over my head. I was awed at the thought of the great and gentle strength represented by the trunks of those huge old trees.

I felt a deep and growing emotion that was thankfulness, and I cupped my palms as if to offer my gratitude, and lifted my heart toward the infinite glory. "Thank you, thank you, thank you," I whispered. "Thank you, thank you, thank you."

At that exact moment, from just above my head, a bird began to sing. And the notes of the song the bird sang were exactly the same rhythmic tempo, each note seemingly echoing my prayerful words. As nearly as I can describe it, the bird sang, "Tweeter, Tweet,...Tweeter Tweet...Tweeter Tweet."

"Mine eyes have seen the glory of the Lord", I said to myself as I opened the door to enter the house where I would begin to prepare to meet the oncoming hours of the new day.

All nature is springing and singing, I thought. We are beginning a new summer, and today is another day the Lord has made in which I will live abundantly blessed by the one who has enabled me to see this garden's beauty and to hear the songs of men and of birds that lead us to thankful praise for all the glory that the Lord has made. It was a glorious morning and I rejoiced and was glad to be in it...

Margaret Taylor Gilmore
June 22, 2004

In the Quietness

Morning wrapped me in a soft gray mist that was almost rain. Gazing upward I felt a comforting confidence in the presence of sheltering trees. I lifted my heart in silent gratitude. And at that moment I distinctly sensed I was in the presence of the holy.

And as I stood in the quietness, awed and alert, I sensed a nearness of other presences. There was a sacredness...a sense of being reassured because I knew...they were the presences of specific individuals whose relationship had made a profound influence for much of what has been for the good in my life...

Experiences such as this have deepened my faith to believe in matters that are mysterious, have increased my gratitude for people who have been a part of my mental and spiritual development, and whose presences seem never to be far away. Those remembered relationships that enriched my life are like strong bulwarks today. Today I am more certain than ever of the power of the influence of those relationships.

Perhaps there is a portion of the eternal presence that is within us all that is more powerful than we have recognized. Could it be there is a part of ourselves that is not limited to restrictions of time or distance? Nor even by death. Could it be, perhaps, that there is a part of the soul of us that is of a dimension known only by heaven's angels and perhaps by individuals who sometimes catch glimpses of certain people whose souls reach out to reassure people they care for. At unexpected sacred moments...they may reach across the vastness to remind us that what we share in friendship with others...out of the most sacred part of us...can continue to be reassuring forever.

What else might explain those unexplainable sudden impressions of being reunited with a fond and familiar presence? Perhaps there is a portion of the very soul of us that is enabled to return sometimes to remind us that the relationships that have made us more aware of the holy do not die with a human death...

Could it be that within a divine plan there is some winged part of the spirit in us...that now and then...is free to return on wings of memory moments to transport a presence who has come back to make someone's misty morning sacred?

Margaret Taylor Gilmore
October 2, 2004

The Mocking Bird's Song

Walking across the parking lot, I heard a bird singing what sounded to me like a "Good Morning" serenade. I had an impression the song was a greeting just for me. I stood still, enthralled, and for a moment I wondered from what direction the melody was coming. Then I saw the mocking bird, almost at eye-level, perched in the exact center of a low gray-green bush, just a few feet away. When I stopped to get a closer look she stopped singing, but I could tell she wasn't going to fly away.

I said, "Well, Good Morning! Thank you! and God Bless you!" The little creature turned her head as though to pay attention to what I was saying. Then it seemed to me she acknowledged my greeting with one tiny "Peep" before beginning again to sing her multi-versed morning song.

I was enchanted, and for the rest of the day I kept thinking that it must be true that when the spirit that lives in the spirit of a human being connects with genuine respect, appreciation and reverence for the created life that is in the heart of a creature,...then there is a sacred sort of mutual trusting, a kind of communication and a spiritual unity between them.

Some of us believe that events such as this prove that there is a wonderful truth known and sometimes actually experienced. It is a miracle of mutual understanding. Some of us call it the kinship of all life. It can happen mostly when we are alone with a creature.

The nesting bird and I shared a mystical moment of mutual understanding. And for a few minutes my heart sang a melody of thankful joy in harmony with notes from the throat of a mocking bird. Even today, remembering that bird, sitting serenely close by an oft' traveled walk, singing from her heart, makes my heart smile.

My experience was one of those "serendipities", one of those wonderful, unexpectedly heartwarming moments that come without our asking. I think they may be just to remind us that God has plenty of extra blessings to give, even when we haven't asked for one.

Consider the mocking bird who is not afraid to sing her morning songs to anyone who passes by her nest. "Free blessings available."

Margaret Taylor Gilmore
March 6, 2002

Thoughts on a Sunday Morning in Late April

En route to "early church" at St. Michael's, I like to drive around The Battery. There I find a comforting, reassuring sense of eternity. Depending on the sky, the water is sometimes blue, sparkling with diamonds as gentle waves stroke the battery wall. Sometimes it is a dull gray hue, the unhealthy shade that marks the character of a white garment that has been washed too many times with dark colors that faded.

Only a few people are out at 7:30 a.m. A few are out to walk their dogs, a few take an early run, some come to sit quietly while dangling a fishing line over the rail of the sea wall.

Visiting "The Battery" early in the morning is almost like being in church. Thoughts are instinctively turned toward things eternal. The water, the sky, the seagulls overhead, and the soft winds that blow across the "timelessness" of it all...these elements invoke one to a contemplative mood.

We who love to visit here early in the morning are mostly very quiet people. Couples walk hand in hand, others will lean on the railing looking outward...some walk alone, their faces meditative as if the solitude is somehow healing.

For me, being on the Battery early on a Sunday morning is somewhat like experiencing a weekly Easter.

Because...Charleston's Battery is more than a historic location, it is a gathering place for meditative souls, and it is a timeless, faith-building demonstration that some things can always be depended upon, such as these tides, skies, Sundays...and Easter mornings' message of triumphant joy.

Margaret Taylor Gilmore
April 28, 1996

White Moth Messenger

It was one of those still moments. It was as if every creature was holding its breath. Listening to the silence, a quietness settled into my soul and eternity seemed very real to me.

Such an experience was mine one day, and afterward I mused that within such moments one can sometimes grasp thoughts that illuminate the far reaches of the place to which we are divinely connected.

I saw what looked a little like a snowflake. Pure white and with a wing spread of probably less than a half inch, the moth was winging a direct course past my window. It was only the briefest of moments and I was still holding my breath when the moth was out of sight.

I thought, "That little creature is alive. It knows where it is going and it knows because God told him how, when and where. So small, so vulnerable...I wondered...where do moths go when strong winds blow?" And how do they know when to go there?

I pray for guidance, protection, provision for my needs. Moths may not pray, but they are guided, protected, provided for and they survive strong winds that would seem too hard for delicate wings to withstand.

Is it that such small things survive because the creator knows where they are and cares...or are moths and butterflies put on earth just to make people wonder?

And I wonder...when crystal pure moments make total silences, are not they perhaps moments when God is holding his breath longing to hear His world thanking Him for life?

Because in the stillness one can hear of secret blessings disclosed. Perhaps within one breathless moment of seeing something too wonderful for words, we may glimpse something we long to see...when all things will be bright and beautiful. It may take your breath away because sometimes even a white moth can seem like an angelic messenger...such moments are often too sacred for words.

Margaret Taylor Gilmore
October 23, 2003

An American Ambassador

The pick-up truck pulled up beside me at the stoplight. From the corner of my eye, I caught sight of something over the top of the cab. The light changed and the truck moved quickly from the left turn lane. It took a bare split second for me to feel a thrill of kinship with the driver. Thankful pride united the two of us.

Attached firmly somewhere near the base of the back of the cab there extended a pole with a very large American Flag. The driver made a brisk and efficient turn and the colors were aloft, rippling in the wind...the colors were fresh and vivid. This was not an old worn flag. This was what appeared to me to be a brand new flag, and it was certainly large enough to give the world a distinct impression of an abundance of thankful pride in America. And it was beautiful to see. I thought how many people would be reminded, and thrilled...just seeing that big flag flying from the top of an ordinary truck

But there is nothing ordinary about the emotions that can come from an individual's heart. Thinking about it, my morning became a bigger blessing. I contemplated the idea that here was an individual who was bold enough to make a bold public statement. Let others think whatever they wish..."This is MY Country's Flag." I think the man was overwhelmed with thankfulness that for a while, at least, the war was over. It was a gesture from his heart.

There is a portion of scripture that says, "Let the redeemed of the Lord say so..." Saying so makes it more so. What we claim aloud becomes stronger, because it is our own voice. I believe that who we claim to be...we are seen by others to be. And the benefits that come are results of that loyalty.

He may be just an "ordinary citizen", that fellow who was driving his truck with the flag flying over his head. But he was, in my book, a top candidate for the title of An American Ambassador to remind every driver on the highway. He made me even more thoughtful, thankful and proud to be an American living in America today. He flew the flag for a lot of us and I thank him, whoever he is...

Margaret Taylor Gilmore
May 2, 2003

Keep a Green Bough

"Keep a green bough in your heart and a singing bird will come." That is the line I remembered this morning when, at dawn, I heard a Mocking Bird singing from his perch on a leafless limb of a tree just outside my window.

I have tried to remember the name of the English professor who said that, but all else I can recall is that sentence, and that she and her invalid mother lived in a small house on one of the shady streets of our small town.

The second part of my remembering is that she had told me she always arranged her mother's food tray using "the best of our china and silver." Somehow those two incidents have lain nestled for many years, deep in my heart's chest of sacred remembrances.

I think I smiled this morning at the sound of the bird announcing to anyone who was listening that in spite of the cold and in spite of the bare tree limbs, that springtime was in his heart.

Then I was inspired to write a note to a friend whom I knew is often overwhelmed with responsibilities and becomes anxious and worried. I told her about keeping a green bough in her heart so that when a singing bird arrived, she would always know that springtimes will always follow wintertimes.

Birds know because God told them so. And they do not worry because God provides their food and He lays it out on the loveliest and best of His tables.

Margaret Taylor Gilmore
February 20, 2003

Bushes That Burn

From across the dark room, it was suddenly there, a very bright, fire-red glow. It flickered like a match that had been struck, but did not burn away. I was mesmerized, because I could not figure out what it was, and though it was small it seemed so strong a flame.

"Like a burning bush," I thought. And I continued to study the sight, wondering, and I grew more puzzled. I stayed seated and waited, deciding to allow the explanation to reveal its origin or purpose in its own time.

The thought came to me that it might be some kind of signal from God. I had just written a paper I had titled, *"A Little Bit Like Moses"*, and thought perhaps that was why the idea of a bush aflame had come to mind.

The little flame continued to flicker, as if caught in some passing wind. I was fascinated and somehow delighted, and a growing eagerness to learn the source of the light that was so alive, so small, and yet so strong.

Then, just moments before morning was about to be born, the mystery was solved. Morning's birth enabled me to see a small glass jar, with a blood red label. This was the light that flamed. The jar was positioned on a shelf so that it was caught in the beam that came from a neighbor's outside light and was being reflected like a brilliant scarlet flame. The flickering was caused by a gentle wind that moved the leaves of trees outside my window.

I was more than satisfied with the solution. I began the day with an impression I had seen a flame that seemed like a personal signal to remind me that I must never forget that wherever I walk, no matter where, I am always on God's holy ground.

Margaret Taylor Gilmore
June 23, 2004

"Prayer Garden" by Alice War

Prayers

Who Am I, God?

I have asked, "Who am I, God?" To answer my own question I have thought...I am who I am to myself...I am my name, I am where I live, I am where I work, I am what people believe me to be. I think, perhaps, that more than all that...I am the individual I am when I write...as I write today.

So what have I to fear in growing older? The identity I fear losing, as I grow older, is the identity that I treasure...that of who, where and what I am...my part in the community in which I have lived and moved for these now many years. Earth born, heaven bound, I am living in another era of questions as to the role of women.

The timeless question I keep asking is, "O sovereign God, creator of all worlds, all generations, all life, in all of this...who am I...to You? I depend on the sufficient mercies of the unknowable power that guides my destiny..., the ever present Holy Spirit, and on the awesomeness of that part of me that stretches eternally outward toward the incomprehensible. Someone has written: "Oh, Lord, be kind to me, the sea is so wide and my boat is so small." Someone else said, "Yes, but never forget that He who made the sea, made you, too."

"Follow...I will follow thee, my Lord...every passing day...My tomorrows are all known to thee. Thou wilt lead me all the way."

Who am I, God? I am listening, Lord.

Margaret T. Gilmore

The Presence

I've been praying, Lord,
and listening.
But how can I know for sure
it's really you when
just before dawn I hear
a bird, along out there,
beginning to sing in the darkness?

I'm alone too, Lord,
listening and praying
that it's really you
nearby, telling that bird
to sing a cheerful song for me.

Is that You, God?
How can I discern
if it's really You
when sometimes I can see
beside the glowing sun,
the moon at midday,
pale, faint, like a fragile memory
of a lovely night, promising
to return again sometime,
somewhere, for me.

"Be still, and KNOW"
is what I hear you say,
"In quietness and confidence
you will find me."
Now I know for sure
that you are both there,
and here, for now I am beginning
to realize that it is in those moments
of waiting and wondering,
praying and listening,
that Your Presence becomes
present to me, revealed
in every bird's song,
every silence, every sunrise,
every fragile moon.

Margaret Taylor Gilmore
September 1, 1998

A Prayer for Blessings before Beginning a Day

I would be true, for there are those who trust me.
I would be giving and forget the gift...
I would be humble for I know my weakness.
I would be brave for there is much to dare.
I would be strong for there is much to suffer.
I would look up and laugh, and love, and lift.

Oh, give me grace to follow my master and my friend.

As certain are the cycles of the seasons, so predictable are the tides of the days of our lives. Each day brings demands, opportunities and responsibilities. Each of us faces our own personal options and opportunities. We are inclined to regard most of our responsibilities as pretty well defined. And so we pray for God's attention and protection as we walk through the day.

Sometimes some of us forget it is alright to pray also for extra, personal blessings. To pray God will bless us is usually our first petition. Following that..."Lord, please show me how to become like a blessing, to someone I meet today, along my way." By thoughtfulness and kindness we speak of God to those who are companions along the way.

Margaret Taylor Gilmore

Song to Welcome a New Day

Touch me with newness, I pray, like a kiss on the lips by a dew drop, falling from a cup of morning. Drench me with dawn, then bind me to you with tender vines that are strong, like flowering ones that nestle close to the trunks of old trees.

Speak softly to me, winds that whisper promises I can believe may be impossibly possible. Stretch me heavenward, Lord, when I face uncertain tomorrows. Help me to remember that it is your breath that fills my lungs with life, and cleans the soil from my blood. Remind me to breathe deeply, Lord, of thy life-giving breath.

Restore me, Lord, I pray, when I wander and wonder why, when I am lost and uncertain and desperately afraid. When I come upon those times of life when I have lost my way, forgetting that all order and system and reason and balance are visible evidences of your timeless plan...Send a someone or a something to remind me.

Help me, O my Father God, when in those hurting times and almost all my breath is gone and almost all my courage has drained away. Help me then, I pray, to remember your promises, then I will stop and listen...and in your mysterious way you will calm my soul and I will breathe your breath. And newness will come, and it will be like a clean wind blowing, restoring reason, orderliness, and purpose into my soul...

And Lord, when my day is over, let me feel your love around me, holding my heart secure, and I will sleep then in the presence of peace.

Margaret Taylor Gilmore
April 22, 2004

All Knowing

As we become ever more eager to know more about you, Lord...we begin to recognize more clearly the precious significance of every person, every seed, every moment's deeds, and the nearer, the more truly, personally more present we know you to be...

Lord, you are all-knowing, all-powerful, all-loving...and it is "your property to always have mercy"...so, Lord, I pray you will accept my poor attempt to express thanksgiving for the uncounted blessings you have showered into my life.

And now, once again...I pray, O sovereign God, that you will hear and answer my daily prayer for protection, direction, inspiration, healing, forgiving, providing, empowering love.

Be ever present to guide my footsteps and strengthen my body, mind and spirit. Be thou in every thought, word and deed, and as long as I live, Lord, let my life be a blessing to others along my way.

And, if it be thy will, O God, grant me a double portion of the gifts I may need to do thy perfect will in my life. Whatever I am, whoever I am in thy sight, please, Lord Jesus, at the end, hold my hand and lead me gently...home.

Thank you, O Lord God, for leading me thus far. I have walked through dark valleys, but you have kept me on my own way to your green pastures. Thanks be to God...for He knows my heart!

Margaret Taylor Gilmore
April 20, 1996

A Child's Prayer

I believe that
a child's prayer is a powerful thing.
A child prays and the Lord listens.
Children pray with simple faith,
and through the purity
of a child's unqualified
trust that God listens, God works miracles.
There is power in the prayers of a child.
I believe that
there is as much power in a child's prayer
as is in the prayer of a pilgrim saint.

Straight to the heart of God
goes the heart of a child at prayer.
And heart to heart, go the prayers
of saints-in-waiting, such as we.
There, in the heart of God
is our source of strength to survive
whatever comes, and sometimes reveals glimpses
of His glory that can make all the difference.
As we have seen in the face of a child who believes
there are angels everywhere and that God always listens.

I too believe, because a part of me is still a child
who trusts that God listens when I pray.

Margaret Taylor Gilmore
November 21, 2001

The Prayer of the Child

When Jesus was a little boy, did His mother teach Him to pray? Were there prayers for children to learn? And in those days when children prayed, how did they pray? And were they sometimes afraid of the dark?

"Now I lay me down to sleep, I pray thee Lord, my soul to keep." That simple prayer might well have been much like those said by children since the presence of God was born into human hearts.

And the prayers children say are pure and with unquestioning belief that God listens. Later on our prayers often hesitate at heaven's gates, feeling unworthy because of our sins and shortcomings. A child's prayer goes straight to the heart of God, and is powerful because it is with pure trust.

I knew of a man who lay dying and praying. And the prayer he repeated again and again was the prayer his mother had taught him when he was a child. "Now I lay me down to sleep, I pray thee Lord, my soul to keep."

I thought, "How beautiful it is that he has returned, finally, to the trust he had as a child, believing in a God whose love promises protection from fear of all darkness, and to those who pray with repentance, assurance that it is God's "property always to have mercy" on His children no matter how young or how old.

During the next twelve months many of us will meet at some point one of our own personal "dark nights of the soul", and perhaps if we can remember then, to keep on praying as a child prays, always placing our soul in God's care, we will be able to lie down and sleep peacefully.

Margaret Taylor Gilmore
December 4, 2001

A Christmas Angel's Message for Little People

Angels and Christmas go together. Earth people and angels sing together at Christmas. Children sing "Away in a Manger." Big people sing "Silent Night, Holy Night" and a really big song, "The Hallelujah Chorus." Angels sing, "Joy to the World."

We think about angels especially at Christmas because there are pictures of them on greeting cards and people put beautiful angels that look like princesses on the top most of Christmas trees.

Christmas angels came to earth to sing of Jesus' birth, but there are other angels who don't always sing...but they carry God's messages that are gifts of love. Usually these angels look just the teacher you like most, or an aunt or a stranger. Sometimes they look like a really good friend of your dad's, or your mom's.

In fact, some of God's very best angels look just like people you already know...Angels often live in people, but even the people don't know it...until another angel visits THEM with a special, unexpected gift that's like a blessing from God. Then they say, "Who? Me?"

Be very still for a little while...Listen, you may hear angels singing...God may be sending you one even now by way of someone you know who doesn't even know that they are an angel. But God has put a good idea in their head, and they are smiling because the thought of making YOU happy makes THEM happy.

But YOU will know, because your heart will help your eyes to see angel's wings while you sing Christmas songs together with all the other people who also know the story of the Baby Jesus.

Grandmother Gilmore
Christmas 2002

Essences of My Thoughts of Worship, Awe and Reverence

No hour is more sacred to me than that of early mornings at home and the Sunday, eight o'clock worship hour at St. Michael's.

Night is done. Light has overcome the dark. And all of earth is waking. I muse that every morning is like an Easter day. "He is risen!" I am alive, and there is possibility and promise in everything, everywhere in all the world.

The very thought that day has arrived exactly on time should be so humbling that we should become silent in amazement and awe. I ponder the beginning of a new day, and gradually become aware that the creator of all worlds is waiting for me to notice Him.

Then, I ask for the presence of the holy to come into all the world that is in my heart. And in the silence of the beginning of the new day I sense a quiet settling in my questing soul.

I prepare for Sunday morning with a feeling of muted joy. Saturday night I begin to think of being in my regular place in St. Michael's, and of the friends and acquaintances who are almost certain to be there too. I lay out the clothing I plan to wear, and fill out the check I will place in the envelope marked with the date. Remembering the descriptions of how Moses directed people to wear the finest attire possible when they prepared to enter the temple, and the generosity of the sacrificial gifts that were brought to be offered in honor of God's love and leadership, I take very personally this careful description of preparation for going to a house built to honor God.

Sundays as I enter the stillness, I feel the presence there, and other awarenesses are diminished. Kneeling quickly and gratefully, sometimes I pray just one word, "Jesus, Jesus, Jesus." For in that one word there is room enough for all the essences that are my distilled praises and enough space to hold my every petition. It feels as if I have heard His voice saying, "I heard you before you asked." And His voice takes away all invasive thoughts of traffic and weather and pains and life's nameless uncertainties.

In the stillness I feel a lingering essence of the prayers of all the people who have knelt where I now kneel. And I hear echoes of all the praise and petitions that have been said by worshippers such as I, in the hundreds of years in that place since. I lift my head to see sunlight streaming through St. Michael's magnificent stained glass window. God is welcoming me. I am safe here, surrounded by peace...

I have long felt it essential that I bring with me some offering, whether it be a tithe or a few coins...A tangible token to symbolize that I have been in this place and have left a something that is a covenant between God and me that means I know

He knows that I am thankful for many blessings, not the least of which is a place called God's house, where I can come and find sanctuary from the noisy world outside its doors...And where His presence will surround me with a welcome, forgiving, and healing love. What I leave in the offering is but "of His own that He has given me."

"In quietness and in confidence shall thy strength be..." Throughout the Bible I find directions concerning ways I should honor God with my life. I find answers when I ask, but sometimes I find questions when I attempt to explain why I believe as I do. It concerns my personal conviction that it is vital to remember that the presence of the holy still "hovers over the deep" and is still in all the world and in all of life. I believe He deserves our attention, in respect, reverence, and awe as we worship.

At times other than morning worship, I have enjoyed the praise and joy-filled, high energy choruses and "glory" songs to which one can clap and tap one's toes to the dance-able rhythms. There are many ways to acknowledge the presence of God. And the first act of that acknowledgment, I believe, is in quiet, contemplative consideration of just exactly who it is before whom we bow our heads, and hopefully, our hearts. My heart is most aware of the reality of the holy in those moments of solitude and silence when the voice I hear is a whisper saying, "Have no fear, for I am here."

My morning prayers at the start of each new day begin with thoughts that are unformed, mixtures, blends and combinations of faces, places, the people I love most of all, and dear acquaintances whose lives are linked with mine in various ways.

From my window I see skies, trees, and sunlight seeping through the blackness of pre-dawn moments. I contemplate how now God has given me another gift-day, with assurance that He has more of life for me to enjoy before the evening comes again.

Gradually my heart reaches out, and up, and my thoughts sweep far and wide. I contemplate my past, my today, and my future. I wonder...what is next, Lord?" And as I pause I begin to remember specific people, and their specific needs, and specific promises I have made to pray come flooding into my mind. My spirit has spoken with the spirit, sometimes in many words, sometimes simply...just one word. And the word my heart dictates is all I need to say to get His attention...is simply the name of Jesus.

Those times of solitudes and silences when I am "practicing the presence of God", are moments of Holy Communion. After having been fed by reading the bread of life, and having sipped from the powerful wine that is in the cup that forgives, protects, directs, and heals, then I am surrounded by angels and prepared for whatever challenge, opportunity or responsibility He has in store for me that day...this life.

Margaret Taylor Gilmore
July 2, 2001

"Floral 1978" by Alice Ward

Poetry

"Dear Lord, take care of me, the sea is so wide, and my boat so small."
(My solace came..."Don't ever forget," He said, "The same God who made the
sea, made YOU...too.")

Promise and Paradise

Gates of heaven,
blaze of glory...
Paradise revealed.

Bridegroom waiting,
Bride of Christ...
almost there...

To be a part of a new, new world,
to be a part of a prism of rainbows,
in a quietly evolving new place,
to be one of God's children.
There...ready to learn and to labor
in a bright, newly created garden...
Eden recovered...
Is a vision too awesome to bear.

What God has in mind for me,
and for those for whom I pray...
may be, must be, Paradise.
Beyond description,
beyond an earth-bound soul's
ability to comprehend.

I believe.

Margaret Taylor Gilmore

I Asked God to Sing Me a Song

I was thinking...Oh, what a wonderful morning this is...I was looking out at a newly washed world. It had been a gentle rain, and soft, slow drops were still falling, causing small rivers to flow, a drop at a time, like slow tears from branches of overhanging trees.

Sing me a song, Lord, I heard my heart saying, sing me a song, tell me it is really You out there in all this glory. And I heard the Lord reply, "Just listen...you will hear me. I will sing for you."

The "other side" of my mind chided me. "How presumptuous can you be...to ask the great God to sing a song, just for you."

But I thought I heard God say, "You wouldn't hesitate to ask a special and talented friend to play a hymn or sing a song for you, why wouldn't it please God for you to ask him to sing for you?"

So, I listened. And I listened. And what I heard was a song the earth was singing. It was a holy moment, and I knew that it was God who was answering with giving me ears to hear Him in the music that is composed in the spheres.

I said, "Thank you, Father God, I hear you singing..." and like my earthly friend who likes to play the kind of songs I like most of all...I clearly heard God singing songs for me...He sang the songs I like most of all. Songs of springtime, creatures calling each other, songs of true thanksgiving, and the song that tells of His love that is forever. And as always, the song God sang to me this morning was blessedly simple, and as always it was awesomely, tremendously grand.

I said, "Thank you, Father God. I hear you and I thank you for not minding when I ask for your special attention...I have heard you sing before, and the words are always the same. They are straight from your heart to mine. Thank you again, because very likely I will ask you to sing that song to me again...tomorrow morning...

Margaret Taylor Gilmore
May 1, 2004

A Tender Power

All things by immortal power
near or far,
hiddenly
to each other so linked are,
that thou canst not stir a flower
without troubling of a star.

These lines, tucked into copies of a friend's sermon notes, caught my attention. Instantly I had the impression of feeling against my hand, the texture of a tender blossom, and the warmth of a star upon my heart.

I searched for further lines from the poem. They were written by an Englishman, Francis Thompson (1859-1907). Perhaps he is best recognized as being the author of *"The Hound of Heaven"*, which he wrote after becoming a priest.

His words, from which the lines above are taken, are from his *"Secret was the Garden."* Those lines, mid-point in the long poem, overwhelmed me with an impression I had discovered the definition of a powerful tenderness that is both earthly and heavenly in its limitlessness.

His poetic themes appear to me to express what his life's experiences had proved to him. He believed that God is everywhere and that He is both tender and strong and further, that the almighty God is both patient and relentless in His efforts to demonstrate in countless interconnected ways, His great love for each of us.

We become reverent as we contemplate the awesome idea that everything is important because every one of us, our every moment, every thought, word and deed matters, eternally, because all of life in all its forms are interconnected.

(Someone has captured the essence of the original version and reworded it this way: "All things in heaven and in earth are linked and thou canst not touch a flower, without causing a star to twinkle.")

Margaret Taylor Gilmore
February 19, 2001

I Love

I love the word, love.

I love mornings and bright sunrises.

I love white lilies and purple pansies.

I love cornbread and peanut butter.

I love mountains and moonlight.

I love sharing lunch and secrets with friends.

I love kneeling at the altar to take communion.

I love how love pulls people together.

I love songs that are gentle.

I love learning old truths that seem new.

I love books and ladybugs and little boys.

I love silk scarves and coats with fur collars.

I love Siamese cats and dogs of any kinds.

I love remembering people whom I have loved.

I love the feeling love does not die when people do.

I love Easter because it causes me to remember...

I love the someone who defied an awesome darkness to prove love does not die with saying so.

Margaret Taylor Gilmore
March 3, 2005

Thanks Be to God in the Morning
Meditation: Memories, Mysteries, Moments and Music

Mountain goats on craggy heights.
A sparrow, alone on a rooftop.

Seas lifting their voices,
chariots in western clouds,
riding on wings of the winds...

Smoking mountains, mists that move,
springs that rise to cause
crystal waters flow beneath little bridges
and sing as they pass pebbles in their path.

Birds and beasts and butterflies,
and suns and snows and fireflies
that play like stars
in soft, dark summer nights...

The mystery of life...
and you...and me.

A galaxy, a rainbow, a four-leaf clover...
We dare to dream and we offer prayers.
And God is always there.

At evening time it's going home time.
At dawn time it is time to go out again...
to experience the adventure of life...

And in Psalm 104 I find this:

"They all look to You
to give them food at the proper times.

When you give it to them, they gather it up.
When you open your hands they are satisfied with good things.
When you hide your face they are terrified.
When you take away their breath, they die and return to dust.

When you go, send your spirit,
then they are created,
and you renew the face of the Earth."

So...who is man that thou art mindful of him...?
And who am I that God can always remember me...protect me,
direct me, inspire me, deliver me and empower me to live
and know the wonders of His love...?

Margaret Taylor Gilmore

The Mystery of Love

The flame burns low.
The glow of remembrance warms the heart.
The eager urgency that marked the joy of the
birthdays of our love is now a precious memory.

So, what is this thing called love?
Like sun and rain and breath and blood,
love is essential to life.

Until life meets life there is no life. And there was
life...after life and it was love...And now there is love
that will forever be...Because life met life one day.
Because God is love.

God's love is indefinable...but it is life...and visible...
"In all around I see...O, thou who changest not...
O, love, abide with me."

The first life-giving flame is now an ember glow. The flesh
grown old, but the spirit is fresher now...more aware,
remembering.

That flame was the light that unbidden, came and saved us
from falling into pits of eternal darkness...when we had
thought we were alone in the night.

"O love that will not let me go...I rest my weary soul in
thee. I give thee back the life I owe, that in thine ocean
depths its flow may richer, fuller be..."

"Ah, sweet mystery of life, at last I've found you...Ah, at
last I know the secret of it all. For 'tis love and love
alone the world is seeking and 'tis love and love alone that
can repay..." Solution. God's love.

Margaret Taylor Gilmore

Moments

.....A cricket, like a noisy clock...ticking off seconds...interrupting my morning meditation...

.....Remembering the strange color of the sky just hours before Hurricane Hugo came ashore...like sheets washing in dirty water.

.....Finding right answers to wrong questions...a mystical phenomenon that continues to reassure me of a reality I had not quiet believed could be true.

.....Silences that sing and silences that are stony...the heart knows the difference.

.....A peace that passes understanding...lines from a song I learned to sing when I did not yet know the difference between peaceful and un-peaceful comprehension.

.....Counting colored beads...a rosary of remembrances of moments that transformed me, and told me I could believe in my most impossible dream.

.....Manna...enough for each day, provided by the spirit that is alive in the Holy Scriptures.

.....Night music...end of day sounds birds make calling to each other...just before stars come out.

.....Memories that bless and do not fade with time because they are made of timeless stuff.

.....Mysteries too marvelous to even try to solve, because they are made out of endless love.

.....Morning, thankful prayers for rest, and petition for protection, direction, healing, and providing and for power to stay on the path toward the Holy Grail.

.....Second hand joy...serendipities...such as when a friend's prayer is answered and she calls to share the depth of her relief and thankfulness.

.....Holy moments...kneeling at the altar, tasting the bread of life...drinking from the cup of salvation.

Margaret Taylor Gilmore
October 2002

Surprises

"God is full of surprises," I said, "I gave two away this week and now I have two more..." My life has been one long adventure, laced through with surprises. Someone else has quoted, "Life is not a test we have to pass. Life is a mystery we must keep trying to solve."

God is a master of mystery, the craftsman of creations, and an arranger of adventures, He is our protector, provider, lover, leader, healer, all-wise, all-knowing, all-powerful to give and to forgive...Christ Jesus is His name, surrounding us with surprises and unexpected reunions, giving us tantalizing glimpses of possibilities that may yet be ours to enjoy in some new tomorrow.

And delighting us now and then with things old that have become suddenly new, like remembered years and the thrills that were our blessings of long ago.

Fifty years ago, a pastor friend gave me a small card with *"The Prayer of St. Francis"* on it. On a morning recently another pastor gave us copies of the same text:

"O Lord, make me an instrument of they peace. Where there is hatred, let me put love; where there is resentment, let me put forgiveness; where there is discord, let me put unity; where there is doubt, let me put faith; where there is error, let me put truth; where there is despair, let me bring happiness; where there is sadness, let me bring joy; where there is darkness, let me bring light.

O Master, grant that I may desire rather to console than to be consoled. To understand rather than to be understood. To love rather than to be loved. Because it is in giving that we receive, in forgiving that we obtain forgiveness, in dying that we rise to eternal life."

This is the Prayer of St. Francis.

Margaret T. Gilmore
March 20, 2001

An April Love Song

Come sit beside me, Love, and together let us sip the wine of early summer. Wine made of a delicious blend of nectar from the dew-washed April flowers.

Come, my April, let us love today and compare this day with other Aprils past. Do you remember Aprils past?

Come, walk with me in the garden and tell me once again that we love because this new April was the one well worth waiting for. Tell me, Love, is this to be my best loved, my most remembered April?

And if, like some loves, this April must depart too quickly into another world, let's not dwell on lost loves...but let our thoughts dwell on our tomorrow mornings when we can watch while May will be getting dressed to welcome June.

Now that is a real love story...April, May and June when lovers pledge and promise to never part from each other.

Come, sit beside me, Love, and remind me that April's love is forever.

Margaret Taylor Gilmore

Mediation on a Morning in May
Come Sit with me Awhile

Come sit awhile with me,
let's share a cup of springtime,
and bask in early morning's light.
Come sit beside me, friend,
let's share this gentle day today,
join me early out here,
for noon time is nearing,
and this fragile springtime
is slipping fast away.
And we always remember forgetting,
that July is never as gentle as May.

Another sturdy summer is out there,
ready and waiting to blaze at dawn
one day, in all its magnificent glory.
And very soon, in June, a thirsty summer sun
will swallow away all of springtime's dew dampened
mornings, mornings so lovely, like this.

So let us fill our cups with the wine of
thanks for this day and celebrate being
bathed in sunlight as we sip the flavor
that is springtime, and raise a toast to us,
as we savor the flavor of friendships
like ours, that lingers like love on our lips.

All the while knowing the boldness of
summer's strong wines will not last.
Then when our summertimes are past,
and autumn's glory is almost all gone,
we will remember mornings like these
when our winter weary souls found
healing and hope, sharing memories,
remembering gentle springtime like this.

So today, my friend, come sit awhile
with me. Let's share one more quiet cup
of morning while we, like springtimes,
celebrate being forever young at heart.

Margaret Taylor Gilmore
May 18, 2004

Snowy Egret

Sentinel still,
solitary, silent
standing in a marsh
green background
for white dignity.

Waiting, watching,
patiently steadfast,
in a quiet place
the egret is at home,
symbolizing quiet antiquity.

Marsh born, sun warmed,
rains fed, his bearing
seems to speak of royal
lineages of wondrous,
lovely winged things.

Sentinel still,
standing there,
the Snowy Egret personifies
the charm, the mystery,
the quiet resolve
and the romantic lore
of the Old South.

Who is it that inhabits
the heart of the Snowy Egret?
I ask my heart...who is it
that manages the marsh,
and makes it home to him?

I wonder if the Egret asks
his heart when I walk by
and wonders things I wonder too?

I think perhaps an angel
standing by, translates
for both of us in the language
of creation's heart of love.

Margaret Taylor Gilmore
1970

Wind Chimes

Sometimes, as they move,
they sing.
Sometimes, as they move,
they are silent.

Sometimes they sing
because I touch them.
Other times they sing
because a vagrant,
small breeze
comes in by way
of an open door...

I watch, entranced,
as they sometimes move
in soundless grace
because I walk past.

Clear, sparkling, shining,
they sing to me in quietness
and I am blessed because
they remind me
of gentle love.

By Margaret Taylor Gilmore
Gladys Irene Fair Taylor's "Little Girl"

The Myrtle Knows

Royalty is coming soon.
Preparing...the Crepe Myrtle tree creates
carpets of lush, watermelon red that are dispersed
by gentle signals in the night.
Millions of tiny blossoms like scarlet snowflakes
settle on streets, doorsteps and paths across
wide lawns.
Some fall into beds of ivy and nestle there,
jewel-like, amid the green, green leaves,
and give illusion...
that the vines have flowered,
magically, since yesterday.

Tall trees and clumps of lower growths
festooned with pompoms of bursting colors...
whites, salmon-ivory, and shades from pinks
to burgundy...
wave in rhythms with sea breezes
and enchant the passers-by.

Crepe Myrtle trees are July's signal
of the approach of autumn's royalty.

(Once, as I walked along my street,
a Myrtle blossom fell into my hair.
It felt, I thought, like an angel's touch.
I smiled,
and walked on...
and left it there,
adorned, as it were,
for royalty.)

Margaret T. Gilmore
July 1990

Somewhere My Love,
Somewhere.

"We'll meet again, don't know where, don't know when,
but I know we'll meet again some sunny day."

Will we meet again? And when did it all end?
Or did it not ever really end at all,
but simply became blended into the strange and unpredictable
tides of time to somehow become a part of eternity's
matchless mysteries...to emerge again sometime,
somewhere...?
Somewhere...my love?

Margaret Taylor Gilmore

Looking Up

Once I was...
Looking up, seldom looking down...
Head up, in the clouds.

Now, head down,
I am "careful, lest I fall."

Once I was unafraid,
running with the winds...
Or straining against the gales...

Years change the way we walk.
Now...I see the ground,
I see the stairs,
And...I miss the stars,
I miss challenging the winds.

Hold my heart, God,
Let me see the distant stars,
let the winds blow,
and let them sing to me.

Let me walk safely
Lord, heart still high,
on rough paths, and on the stairs.
Hold my hand now, Lord,
let me walk safely, and unafraid...
Through the shadowed ways,
just as you have
kept my steps secure
on the stairs and
through the years,
that have bowed my head,
and slowed my steps,
but not my heart.

Margaret Taylor Gilmore
June 12, 2001

Thanksgiving 1995

Thanksgiving.
Mixed emotions.
Thanks versus no thanks.
Wishing days were longer.
Wishing they'd leave TIME alone.
Wishing I could stop the clock
for a little while until
my heart is ready for
next year.

Thanksgiving.
Coming too soon this year.
I'm not ready yet
to be truly thankful
because "It'll soon
be Christmas."

This year, like me,
is too soon old.
Perhaps I'm too late to start
to appreciate November
this year the way I ought.

I must have missed something
since last Thanksgiving Day.
Just yesterday, I recall,
we were calling
to each other, saying
"Happy New Year."
That was before Before.

Has it been a happy year?
I suppose it was
for I remember little
of the hours of the days
because the "present" escaped
me...mostly
because I felt alone.

Was it because
I forgot to notice
so much of Life
and its blessings.

And walked sightlessly
through the months
thinking only...
of myself?

Or am I pensive now
because I want to forget
that Thanksgiving's arrival this year
means the ache I've tried to ignore
isn't going away
when THEY do?

Margaret Taylor Gilmore
November 1995

"Wildflowers" by Alice Ward

Seasons,
Easter and Christmas

Just Before Morning

As his lungs exhaled for the last time, his body relinquished its effort to willingly continue to submit to pain. There was a moment of darkness, then a quiet voice spoke and he slipped into a profound silence without answering. He did not feel the sword that slashed through his side. Nor did he feel the water and the blood that flowed from the wound.

He did not waken when the nails were removed and he was taken from the cross. He did not stir when firm and gentle hands removed the blood stains from his brow and feet and nor did he know when he was wrapped in clean, dry garments and positioned on a low shelf in a cave.

His "crown" had fallen to the ground and where it fell, the feet of the soldiers pressed it deep into the soil and a thorn of it took root and grew. The sprouting tree was not noticed until the men decided to move the next crucifixion to another location. Only until months later did someone notice the crown sprouting green. Strangely, no one thought it significant.

Except Barabbas, who sometimes walked there to reflect on his part of the story. His life had also been changed by Jesus' death. Every day he thought how close he had come to be the one crucified.

Jesus did not know the moment when strong men rolled a great stone into place over the mouth of the cave, and for several hours there were no sounds anywhere except the yawns of men who had been ordered to guard a dead man's grave.

For a while, he felt nothing, because he was beginning to heal. Deep, restorative healing was washing over him. Then there was a gradual knowingness that brought an impression that a new morning was about to dawn. And the faint light began to enable him to see his mother's face. He paused to smile because the joy in her face was the same he had seen when thirty-three years ago she gazed lovingly down at him, lying in the manger.

He heard soft sounds, like wings brushing past and over and around him, and then the quiet voice brought him to full attention. He felt strong again, clean, ready, and the voice spoke of other days, other worlds, some past, some yet to come. It was as if he was hearing his own voice and he rose, walked to the stone that had sealed him inside the tomb. With his touch, it moved smoothly aside.

It was at that time when Easter began to be celebrated. And the chorus that sang that morning was the same angel chorus whose song startled those shepherds on that night when Jesus had been born in Bethlehem.

Then Jesus lifted his eyes and saw heaven's glory....and then a vision came to him of other worlds that needed love, some new, some old, and he saw more wandering people. But he knew love is powerful and he remembered how some people had seen his life and his love and his suffering and it had changed their lives forever. He was glad because He knew some of the people who had seen how the power of love can move away the biggest stones and they had never stopped telling the story. Easter is love and love is Easter's message. Easter is a song about stones that can be moved away by the powerful touch of love.

Margaret Taylor Gilmore
February 29, 2005

Perhaps It Happened This Way

His foul breath and his spittle made her shrink from it with every sensitivity in her body. She could even smell the odor of the men who were taking him to where he would be tried.

And when he felt the blows and stumbled as they pushed him along, she felt in her own body even the small pain made by the scrape on his shins made by even the smallest stones.

And when he was lifted to the sky, and everyone could see his body hanging there, the pain she felt was the kind of pain only a mother can feel. Because the child to whom she had given birth would always be, in his flesh, a very real part of her own body.

Nothing could erase her memories, nor anything separate her body from that of the son she knew had been conceived without a seed from a human father.

And as she followed him all the way and wept, her body felt his agony as if it were her own. There was no human father to hold her as she wept, no one who could feel what she was feeling in her body and in her heart. She had known it would happen. She had tried to believe it would not come to this.

They had been together in many experiences as he grew to manhood and became the man he had been destined to be. She knew from the first this boy would always make a difference wherever he was. She had shared her wonderment with Elizabeth when they were both pregnant with the sons both of whom would ultimately be killed because they were different from other men.

But neither of them knew just how very different those boys would grow up to become. And there came days when they wished their sons could have been less "different."

And on this final day of Jesus' earthly life, his mother's pain was as exquisite as any loving mother could ever possibly feel. The part of her body that was still a part of his body that was able to feel as a human being feels...she knew that they were still together in body, mind and spirit. They were sharing a kind of mutual agony beyond mortal bearing...and she wept for the thought that this was the hour he would leave her forever.

But at that moment she saw him turn his face toward a disciple standing at the foot of the cross and she heard him say to him, "Take care of my mother." Then she felt a peace beyond understanding. She had finished what she had promised when she had responded to the voice that had told her she had been chosen to become the mother of the one whose life would give peace to all people who asked Him for it. Now she understood and she was finally willing to let Him fulfill the task He had been sent to do.

At that moment, the earth convulsed as in an earthquake. The sky darkened and thunder and lightening sent the crowds scattering for shelter. The mood of the celebration of killing was changed and they dispersed to go back to town where they would tell each other what they thought had happened. Some knew who had died that day. Many did not.

It is a story beyond understanding, and worthy of believing.

Margaret Taylor Gilmore
March 4, 2004

She Ran to Tell the Truth

She ran as fast as she could down the rough mountain path toward the town. Dawn had not yet broken, but she was barely aware of the hard stones she could not see that lay beneath her tender feet.

She couldn't wait to tell what had happened to her. Something had awakened her, and in the earliest hour since midnight she had risen from her bed to go where Jesus' body lay buried. There to simply touch the stone at the mouth of the tomb, and be as near to Him as was now possible. But something else had happened and she couldn't wait to tell everyone that she had found His tomb was empty...

She ran and she ran, and when her lungs began to tell her she should not continue to strain them, she ignored the knowing, and kept on running until she flung open the door to the house where her family still lay sleeping.

"He's alive, He's alive, He's really alive", she shouted. "Wake up, let me tell you what happened to me up there on the mountain." Everyone was startled awake and even more than amazed when she described why she knew for certain the identity of the man she had seen. "I know it was Jesus, because He knows my name."

Some people wondered, some people doubted. And some believed what the young woman described was true. They discussed it with each other, "Remember? He told us He would die, and then return some time. Remember? Is this not the third day since they killed Him? Now...what are we to do, now that we know? Will He return to us too, and if we see Him, will He tell us about death so that we can understand?"

Then the young woman, who was the first person to have seen death defeated by love personified, went out alone to a quiet place where she planted a tree. And soon it became a tradition in the town because people started to notice that every springtime after that, the little tree always burst into bloom on the morning of the day known to us as Easter.

Margaret Taylor Gilmore
Easter 2005

The Road to Emmaus

I have not had a road to Damascus experience, but I have walked the Emmaus Road. Sometimes the road of life is strewn with stones of sorrow, deep ruts of disappointments, clumps of muddy confusion and heavy rocks of remorse. I have walked that road and sometimes I have wandered, weary and wavering in my sense of direction as I tried to "keep the faith."

Today I know had I stopped to really notice, I might have recognized events along my way that would have given direction, soothed my troubled thoughts and eased my aching heart. Now I know there have been "ordinary glimpses of glory", events and individuals I looked on at first as ordinary, everyday things I took for granted.

Today I am more serene, remembering unexpected moments, people, sounds and sights that eased my pain and diverted discouragement. Once, when I entered a room in a house I had not visited before, I suddenly caught the lovely scent of lilacs, arranged on a table near the door. Suddenly, tears began to flow because memory had swept me back in time. I was no longer a grown woman with a hurting heart...I was a girl, young and safe, in my grandmother's home where lilacs bloomed faithfully every springtime.

And on another aching afternoon I was strangely soothed, coming upon a little mountain stream running over mossy rocks. Sitting there, listening to the water's music, my heart was lifted and I knew I was no longer lost, but very sure that my guide knew exactly where I was that day, along my Emmaus Road of life...

There have been angels, too. People who appeared at exactly the right time with exactly the right ability, prepared and willing to supply the exact kind of help I was so desperately needing at that moment. My heart soars with gratitude at such times and a rainbow shines into my spirit's eyes.

I am reminded at such times of what happened to those dejected disciples trudging toward Emmaus, thinking all their dreams had died. But along the way, a mysterious stranger appeared, and afterward when they had finally recognized who He really was, they said to each other, "Don't you remember, how our hearts grew warmer when He came and talked with us?"

Thereafter their road ahead became no longer a flight from fear and lost hope, it became a challenge to walk the rest of their lives with confidence, because they had met the man who knew from personal experience about every hazard that can come along the way of every pilgrim's life. But it is the road that ultimately leads home.

Margaret Taylor Gilmore

Barabbas

When the guard started unlocking his chains, the chilling thought came to him that this was the day he was to be taken to the place where they would crucify him. Sick with terror he drew back, and was astonished that the guard did not turn to drag him along. Every nerve in his body was crying out in terror. He had seen them crucify men, so he knew what lay ahead. Other prisoners watched silently because they too knew.

When the guard unlocked the prison gate and said, "Go!" he thought it was another way to torture him, tempting him to try to escape. But when he was shoved forward, then heard the gate being locked behind him, his feet took wings and he ran. He bolted into the street and ran as if pursued by lions. And then he ran until his chest felt as if it would burst.

"It must be a test," he thought. "They are trying a new way to torture people. See how far and how fast a prisoner can go, trying to escape, to see them too exhausted to fight back when they begin to drive the nails, then the real torture act can be even more exciting. I can't run much further they will catch up with me soon."

But he kept on running, breathing hungrily of these brief moments of freedom. Then, gradually he began to wonder, though it was midday, why there were no people in the streets. And he became aware of loud voices coming from a distance. The sounds were like those he had heard when he had been near an arena where gladiators were fighting. He remembered how he could almost feel death's presence in the air, and it was in the air here, now.

Then, just a little way ahead of him, he saw an old man, sitting in front of a potter's place. As the runner slowed in front of the old man, their eyes met and the runner saw that his eyes were not old, and that the old man was not afraid of him, even though it would be plain to figure someone running like that would be an escaped prisoner.

"Why are there no people?" the runner asked. "Where are all the people?" "They are at the celebration on the hill," the old man replied. "What celebration?" the runner asked. "You must not have been around this town lately," the old man said. "They've got the fellow they say has been trying to take over the government. They are crucifying him today." And the old man proceeded to explain all he had heard about the man who had caused such an uproar among the people.

"They say Pilate wasn't ready to put the fellow to death, because he was curious about him. He had wanted to talk with him because it had been reported he had claimed to be The Truth. Pilate wanted to see if that was actually what this strange man had said...

"And besides that, what kind of criminal would walk willingly, straight into the middle of the crowd of men who came to arrest him?"

"Pilate was being pressured to crucify Jesus. But his curiosity made him decide to offer the crowd an alternative prisoner. It was his custom to now and then set a prisoner free. He offered, because it would satisfy the crowd, perhaps, and give him another opportunity to examine Jesus.

The old man continued. "It is one of those things governors do sometimes, just to demonstrate their power over the life and death of people under their jurisdiction. So sometimes there are contests for the people to choose one of two criminals who would be set free, just to entertain the crowds."

The runner had stopped wanting to run. He wanted to hear what else the old man had to say, and strangely he was no longer afraid.

"Pilate knew there were already two other men who were to be crucified that same day, and after all, did it really matter who it would be? But the crowd would accept no substitute. This fellow, Jesus, had done strange things, and it had been hard to figure why he kept on submitting to abuse and never once complained. So they set a man free, a fellow named Barabbas, even though he'd been caught trying to start a revolution against the government."

The old man was enjoying the conversation, because he was all but certain he knew who it was to whom he was explaining the events of the past days. He told all he had heard about Pilate's offer to send another prisoner to take the place of Jesus, but that the crowd's thirst for blood was directed toward Jesus. It was because he was a different kind of prisoner, and his submissive manner whetted their curiosity. This was their chance to watch the man they thought might perform one of those miracles some people said they had seen him do.

Meanwhile on the hill, there were some in the crowd who achingly hoped Jesus would do something to save himself, and prove he was truly who he said he was. But most of them wanted to see what he might do that was different from other men being crucified. But being different was the problem...not just somewhat different, but truly different. This man was so different he made some people feel it was they who were different and it made them feel as if it were they who were doing something wrong.

It was that, and the way he had kept telling people that what he said was truth...and that was why they felt they had to get rid of him. That word truth and the man's humility made them uneasy, so no substitute criminal would do.

"That was the problem," the old man said. "The word Truth makes people feel uncomfortable. Truth is a word that takes a truth to describe it. And claiming to actually be the truth was a dangerous thing to say."

Then the old man watched as the runner walked away. He walked as a man walks when he has a purpose and a place and a promise to keep. Now Barabbas knew who he was. And he knew the name of the man who was willing to die so that he could have a new kind of freedom...Barabbas knew it was a miracle he could not explain, but he could not wait to tell the story the old man had told him...about himself, a redeemed sinner.

Great waves of emotion surged through his body, his mind, his soul. It was as if he had been caught in the center of a great cataclysmic, cleansing storm. It had cleared him of all the confusion, anger, the hurting and explained the longing for something he had not known how to find during all his years.

Jesus did not know Barabbas, but he had been willing to die in his place. Now Barabbas knew why the prison gates had been unlocked so he could go free. It took a miracle he didn't deserve, but Jesus had died, willing to do so because God knew there would always be men like Barabbas who would need to be told that it is true that there is a someone who is willing to die for people like him...

Barabbas was no longer a rebel, nor a guilty criminal. He went to the river, washed himself clean of prison soil, and then went to his home where he had not gone for many years. His mother saw him coming and she wept for joy. "I am home, and I am clean," he told her. "Because a man named Jesus died today so I could live free and forgiven."

His father asked, "Tell me more about this Jesus. If He has changed your life, perhaps He can change mine too..."

Margaret Taylor Gilmore
March 21, 2004

Early Easter

Easter came for me this year in late March. It happened this way.

First, plundering through a folder of old letters, I found a lavender envelope containing three pressed stems of fragile green leaves and on each small stem was a delicate lavender woods violet.

Suddenly I was four years old. I was holding my grandfather's hand as we walked through a wonderfully green and wooded place. Suddenly, seeing a clump of tiny lavender flowers, I let go of his hand and ran to gather a handful to take to grandmother, I told him.

And as I touched the violets in the envelope, I was reminded of the day I had found the almost hidden clump of lavender violets at an unlikely place beside a highway rest stop.

I had felt a reverence in the presence of that place, because of the violets and the memory they evoked. Carefully, I cupped them in my hands and carried them all the miles home to place them carefully between pages of a book. It was as if I had found proof my memory of that springtime day when Grandpa took my hand and led me to a place where I saw something for the first time that I had always remembered had made my heart leap for joy.

And then...this very morning...my heart was filled with an Easter feeling when I saw three wonderful sights that took my breath away. They were so very THERE, overnight, and I had not seen them the morning before.

First was an unusually large clump of wisteria hanging at the edges of a tree limb. I have lived in this house for several years, and have never seen wisteria growing in that part of the garden. It was elegant, it's white with lavender contrasting the trees, greener than ever, just having been washed by early morning mists.

Next, a strange tree in the garden is oddly spectacular because of its gangling shape. Sometimes I think it knows the others think it ought not to be there. It is not an ordinary tree and not at all a pretty tree, especially when bare. This year I had been horrified to see someone had pruned it back so severely I thought it was probably going to die. Just a few days ago I had looked again at it and was sad because I thought it still had the look of death. But this morning that tree was a dramatic sight...every part of every stubby branch was alive, covered with white blossoms. I said, "Oh thank you God, for bringing that tree back from what I feared was death."

My third Easter affirmation is a tree that nobody had planted. It had grown outside my window, spreading itself gracefully, and was framed by a corner window of my living room. I loved that tree, because for years I had found great

me. And sometimes they came close and stayed for a little while, as if to watch me.

enjoyment, watching red birds gather on its branches to sit and sing there...for me. And sometimes they came close and stayed for a little while, as if to watch me.

I loved that tree and was heartsick when most of its limbs were broken off in one of our hurricanes. For a year or so, what I could see from that window had no resemblance to the graceful branches I so loved. This Easter morning, "my tree" had brought out its leafy life, seemingly overnight, and had formed a leafy curtain, almost as much as it had done before the storm.

I was thankful that after the storm no one had decided to cut it all the way down, but had ignored the stump and so a few branches remained and the broken tree drank deeply of the earth and managed to live again.

And so it was, that for me, Easter came almost a month before the calendar said it was due. For me springtime has come into my soul just like I think it did in Eden...it came as a blessed surprise. Easter mornings arrive for us according to God's arrangements. And beautiful things happen to people and to trees and birds and little flowers when it is exactly the right morning...Easter makes hearts sing when God says to his creation, "Come...it's time to rise and sing for joy..."

And that is why now I am celebrating Easter every morning, especially in springtime.

Margaret Taylor Gilmore
March 31, 2003

An Easter Morning Worth Waiting For

He was a retired Admiral. He was "tough." He didn't suffer fools gladly. He had served America in a significant way, especially during World War II. He was connected, politically, socially and by blood kin, with individuals in high places of this government. He'd been born and raised according to the beliefs of his father's traditionally solidly grounded Anglican church. However, as soon as he left home to attend a prestigious university, he left church attendance out of his lifestyle.

He challenged every rule, and managed to become exceedingly popular with intellectuals who saw in him the potential to be an effective, strongly motivated leader. For a while he was a Navy test pilot. Later, he was put in charge of matters vital to this country's winning the conflict in Europe.

He married well. His wife was born into a family whose name was recognized all across the country. She fitted well into the social scene where there were people whose names were familiar in Washington and across Europe.

They were a couple whose politics were well known also because her brother was a candidate for President of this country. He lost, but the couple remained close to people who frequented the White House.

After the war was over, President Truman sent her brother and her husband, the Admiral, on a peace tour across the world. It was clear there were strong ties among men who were graduates of the same universities.

The world peace tour was an experience that provided extensive media coverage and left the Admiral with memories sufficient to give him a valuable first hand insight concerning the characteristics of individuals who, in the years afterward became politically recognized in this country and in other parts of the world. Thus he was able to be a keen evaluator of world politics.

After they retired, his wife died suddenly and the Admiral was left with his big house, his bulldog, Rocky, and his memories. I did not know until months afterward what had become of her ashes.

As he reached his mid-eighties, his eyesight diminished further and his world became smaller. The man who had walked with kings and world leaders began to speak more about his own life experiences and to contemplate the future of politics in the hands of another generation.

When he was asked which world leader he would guess might start the next world conflict, his prediction was astonishingly accurate.

He said, "I don't think a world leader will start the next war, I am afraid it will begin by way of a surprise attack set off by some crazy zealot.

I thought of my friend, the Admiral, on that fateful morning when I heard the Twin Towers had been the target of the anger that was in the heart of one obscure individual. And I believe he would have had some specific ideas as to what should be done by this country. He was a true patriot.

Age diminished his body, but not his mind. One day he shared what he had done with his wife's ashes. I had not asked because Admiral was a private person and hadn't seemed willing to talk about what he believed concerning things holy. Once he had asked his housekeeper what she believed about Jesus and such matters. She said after she had told him, he nodded and then went to his room saying he believed he needed a nap.

One morning just after Easter he told me he had kept the ashes until Easter week drew near. Soon after she died, he had made arrangements with a friend who owned a helicopter. The pilot was to take the urn aloft. Then just as the morning sun rose above the Virginia mountains, the pilot was to pour the ashes from the urn so that they would fall over the place where the Admiral and his wife had lived and loved during the early years of their marriage. The Easter morning breeze would waft them downward, like soft silver dust, to settle again into the earth.

I had known there was a part of the Admiral that was sensitive. I had caught glimpses of his softness when he described certain events concerning his wife. And the vulnerable part of him became very clear when his beloved old bulldog had to be put to sleep. "Don't mention Rocky to him," his housekeeper said. "He can't handle that subject right now."

I had glimpsed the part of him that he seldom allowed the public to see. But I had not known there was such a deep part of him that was so romantically and spiritually strong until I saw it clearly when he told me what he had arranged for that first Easter morning after his wife had died...

When I learned the Admiral believed waiting for Easter was the right way to express his last good-bye and "I love you" to his wife, it was then I knew he had returned to embrace the faith of his father's teaching.

My heart is lifted to a daybreak morning every time I think of the Easter story the Admiral told me.

Margaret Taylor Gilmore
October 30, 2003

Forever Springtime

There it lay on the damp green grass,
a small, three-pronged sprig of gold leaves,
tinged with green. I bent down, picked it up
and holding it by its slender stem,
I felt strangely, deeply reverent.

It's true, I thought, summer is gone,
springtime is gone, and this morning
I'm holding autumn in my hand.
And another winter is sure to come.
I love my sprig of autumn...it makes
me feel wistfully youthful and wonderfully
worshipful...I have carefully pressed the lovely
leaves between pages of my Bible.
Now the soft dampness of the rain that had
washed them and the life that had remained
in them is all gone.

I have made a photo likeness of the sprig, and
the process shows no gold nor green, but what it
did reveal was the lovely, fragile skeletal
outlines within each leaf. The sturdy stem on which
they grew clearly shows the orderliness of each
separate leaf, perfectly positioned in its own place
among the others.

Today I have captured in my thoughts the seasons
of nature and of life...In my hand I have held
the subtle essences of springtime, summertime,
and autumn. The sprig of gold I found
I look upon as a symbol to remind me of the
sacredness of things that are forever, eternally
timeless, beautiful, priceless and promising.
In the pressed and dried green and gold,
I have glimpsed memories of my own life's
sweet springtimes and my evolving summertimes,
and am reminded of how many times that the
arrivals of autumntimes have surprised me.

And only now have I begun to really contemplate
the inevitableness of wintertime. But...within the drying

sprig of gold and green, I sense a promise that springtimes are forever.

Margaret Taylor Gilmore
September 25, 2002

Contemplating Easter Day

Winter is past. Earth's face is turning toward the sun. On a morning soon, many people will rise early to go to some quiet place out of doors where they will meet others to watch the sun rise on another Easter day.

In the quiet of an early Easter morning, we may glimpse fresh concepts about the business of being alive. And as we contemplate, at some moment we may become aware it is God's own breath that is filling our lungs with fresh supplies of life. And we discover again that being reminded of the meaning of Easter can be an exceedingly emotional experience.

Later at the church trumpets will sound, and the white-robed choir will march in, following the cross. Then everyone will sing, "He arose, He arose, Christ arose." Few could deny Easter morning can bring our emotions to a depth that is difficult to describe. We find it interesting to contemplate Jesus' rising from the tomb was somewhat as if He had been born again.

Consider this...we are all born again when we arise every morning. The darkness is gone and we are turning our faces toward the light of a new day. God has brought us through the night and kept our lungs filled with life, even when we did not know it was His love that kept us alive while we slept.

The sun rises somewhere every morning, and for some people Easter is the most beautiful morning of all days because they believe in a place called somewhere, everybody they have ever loved and lost for awhile, will be singing, "Easter is another way God wants you to know that love does not die when people do."

Margaret Taylor Gilmore
For Easter 2005

December 26, 2005

Sunday morning was sunny, but a bit brisk. Entering church and just inside the vestibule, we stopped to watch on a small monitor a live video of St. Michael's tower. We stood fascinated. The screen was showing nine bell ringers preparing to tug nine tremendous bells toward earth to bring to us and to the city, a call to worship. At a given moment, the leader signaled and then in rhythmic precision, the bells rang out and thus began the pealing of their powerful voices. We were told the bells are so heavy they could lift a ringer heavenward if not carefully handled. We heard precision and promise in their clanging might, and it was glorious. Because for us this was the day they rang in praise with us, and it was on such a day as this...on such a day as this Christmas.

After a while, I could no longer bear what was filling my heart with thanksgiving, nor keep my eyes from overflowing with awe. All that I could say as I prayed was, "O, thank you, thank you, thank you, Heavenly Father. Thank you for these bells. Thank you for this day, this place, for EVERYTHING...Thank you."

Then as the processional began and the great gold cross passed our row, followed by the robed choir and the leaders who would lead us in words of confession, praise and thanksgiving, I felt emotion straining my throat again. Then settling in to listen as scripture was being read, and joining in singing the familiar carols of Christmas...I thought the bells and the procession and the flowered altar had said it all for me. But just then, from the balcony behind us, a member of St. Michael's began to sing without accompaniment. This is a woman whose voice has a tone that matches the great bells...Ever so slowly, ever so reverently, she sang a simple song. "Go....tell it on the mountains, go tell it on the mountains and everywhere, that Jesus Christ is born today..."

I had a distinct impression that even to whom those words are familiar...many people found themselves unexpectedly stunned by a strong renewed awareness of what the song says...

At the end of her final note, I knew the people wanted to applaud, but were instinctively restrained and totally quiet. Awe had taken charge of the moment. Some sensed, some knew the singer had poured her heart and soul into her voice and she had sung with the sort of inspiration that comes only rarely in times and in few places.

I heard her as one who hears a familiar song for the first time, but the moment was too awesome to last. I didn't want her song to end. Today I have a longing to tell someone how deeply she moved my heart as she sang the message of Christmas for us...

Afterward, I shared a meal such as might have been prepared for royalty. Because I was at a table with friends who had become even dearer because we had shared that sacred hour in worship and had knelt together at the altar in the act of praise and petition, partaking of the symbolic body and blood of the one who brought us together in celebration of His birth.

That is why I knew I needed to make a written record to be read by someone, some day...my account of how, this year, Christmas day brought me a full and running over cup of thankful joy.

I told my friends, "Christmas for me, can't get any better than this..." Unless... perhaps...Christmas is a day set aside in eternity...to be celebrated with all the company of heaven...

Margaret Taylor Gilmore
December 26, 2005

My Left-Over Christmas

Today is January 4, 2006. Christmas is over. Now what shall I do? What shall I do with what is left of my Christmas?

I survey the clutter of my house where there is a lot of Christmas left over in red bows and ropes of greenery. And there is the already beginning a feeling of guilt because I owe so many letters. Now I am faced with knowing I will have to remember those yet to be written letters of thanks for gifts, messages written on cards and calls waiting to be returned, preserved on the answering machine.

And what do I do now, Lord, with all those left-over bows and boxes and bowls of left-over festive food, too delicious to let go to waste. And there is a large accumulation of candy and cookies, decorated with little trees and little holly berries. Who lives near to me that might NEED cookies?

What do I do now, Lord, with Christmas? A book of humorous quotes has a page at the end with a tired-looking creature pictured saying, "It was lovely, but I have to scream now." I don't feel like screaming, Lord, but where am I to store away all the NEW symbols of Christmas I've accumulated since last year's Christmas? This morning as I began to try to find room for the objects around this house that are too precious to risk damaging by careless "putting out of sight", I thought, "Perhaps there is room in that upper closet.," But there I found a huge box of decorations from years past. If I'd remembered, I might not have felt the urge to purchase anything more this year.

I'd simply been too busy preparing for this year's Christmas, and too absorbed in meeting other deadlines to remember decorating for Christmases past. And now, just a week later, I had begun to forget Sunday morning and the glory of celebrating Christmas day at my church. I'm sorry, Lord. Please forgive me for forgetting so soon how blessed I am.

But...at this point this day, I am becoming even more weary of trying to deal with my left-over Christmas, and wondering how I could ever find my way out of the impossible task of coping, sensitively, reverently...with my left-over, pent-up frustration.

But there has come a gradual dawning of remembrance of a Christmas gift that was the one that touched me the deepest. It is an exquisite, crystal clear, blue/silver cross. It is a perfect size to hold in my hand, and it feels solid, strong and as if it knew from its beginning that it would belong to me. It is Christmas to me. I believe this special cross was destined from the beginning to interpret Christmas for me...

Today it is secured by a small suction cup to hang just above my head in a window in my kitchen. My friend placed it where light will shine through it by day and by night when there is light from any source, by moon or by stars.

Now I know what to do with my left over Christmases...I will always know it is a holy season, remembering that Christmas day is symbolic of the first chapter of the story that tells about the birth of Jesus. And my beautiful blue/silver cross is a symbol of the kind of love that will not ever let me stray far from remembering I am loved, because He loved me enough to prove it by dying on a cross. Now there is nothing in me that was my left over longing to be assured I am loved.

Margaret Taylor Gilmore
January 4, 2006

"Tomorrow" by Alice Ward

Tomorrow's Journey

Geese...En route to a Better Pond

I was on my way toward the gates that separate the campus from a major highway intersection. I wondered why the cars ahead of me had stopped just past the gate, then began very slowly to move onward toward the traffic light. Soon I saw the reason. It was a flock of Canada Geese, going out through the gates, and strolling toward the open highway. It was almost five o'clock in the afternoon, and traffic was heavy.

I wondered what had caused them all to leave the Reflection Pond at the center of campus where they had been for several weeks. Whatever it was, those geese were apparently looking for another place to settle. I worried, but I had no choice but to keep going because there were cars behind me. And I asked myself what could I have done, anyway?

This morning I woke, my thoughts filled with a mixture of thoughts about the geese yesterday and remembrance of brief and sketchy dreams I'd had last night. One dream was about my grandmother, a quiet, patient and gentle lady who took me as her own when my mother died. She taught me little songs, among them one that came to my thoughts this morning. "Go tell Aunt Ida, go tell Aunt Ida, go tell Aunt Ida the old gray goose is dead." Somehow the straying Canada Geese and that old song combined and an idea formed in my thoughts.

Lately my instincts have led me to longing to see loved ones who have gone on ahead of me into the great unknown. Unbidden, their faces have come to my memory and I have become less apprehensive and more eager to see what lies beyond the familiar pond and the speeding highway traffic of life, where I am gradually becoming less and less self confident.

Perhaps I am like one of those geese, headed toward a destination that may seem dangerous, but drawn in that direction because I believe there is more water, more life beyond the great highway I'm thinking I must cross.

Some day someone may say, "Go tell someone...Go tell someone, go tell them she's gone...she dared believe there is a better place for her to go...she crossed the highway safely, and she's gone..." was within me...somewhere. The knowing that now I know that I know is like a release to know.

Margaret Taylor Gilmore
August 23, 2002

Epiphany

I have found it, I have found it! The answer I have always known. I have found the beginning of the end of the chapters of the story of my life. I have glimpsed the dawning of the day of my destiny and the sky is pink and gold and the palest of blue. October is over and I am in the November of my life.

Advent and Epiphany are happening in me, and I am rejoicing. For each new day is a day the Lord has made, especially for me. The vague, rich and spicy scent from my spent summers and Septembers lingers and drifts by me, and the once burning questions to which I once felt I had to find perfect answers are only embers now...because I know enough now, to know that I know enough.

I think now that it is as if I am experiencing my own Advent season of life. Because I am at last preparing to be content to accept end things. My physical body has spoken quietly, saying it needs more rest. And in my dreams I wander the universe and converse wordlessly with interesting people I cannot remember when I awake.

I find I am thinking more often now of being a part of the ages than being a part of the on-goingness of today's world. Now and then when I am alone I speak aloud, practicing greetings I will say to loved ones long gone. And I find myself smiling to think of them, each greeting me as if I've just come home after a long journey.

The ever-circling years have come around again, and there are memories of melodies of new-old songs, such as angels might sing, ringing in my ears. Advent season is here and I find I am experiencing my Epiphany and it is lovely.

Margaret Taylor Gilmore
August 16, 2001

Ponds and Pebbles

I tossed a pebble into a pond and meditated as I watched the widening of the first small circle of ripples my pebble had made. Then my imagination translated the sight and it was as if my pebble was a prayer I had made. I saw in my mind the circle of ripples widen until it reached the outermost edges of the place where prayers reach the heart of God.

The pond, I thought, is the world of our years. We are forever tossing pebbles. Little acts, sometimes thoughtful, sometimes thoughtless, some carefully considered, some hasty. Some pebbles are words of thanks, sometimes a smile. Sometimes we pray frantically, tossing large stones of petition. Sometimes we pray and toss pebbles that skip across the top of the water. These are pebbles of joy when wonderful things happen. Watching the pond's surface and the ripples that widened caused me to ponder, could it be that as the ripples widen, would they not at some point become a part of other ripples from other prayers, and would it not result in wider circles and give glimpses of how endless is the expanse of eternity's waters? And I wondered how powerful are those pebbles that we toss?

There are many pebbles in my pack of prayers. Each morning as I pray, each pebble apart, one person at a time, one praise, one petition at a time. Sometimes I wonder how deep it will go, and how long will it be before the last prayerful ripple widens until it reaches the shore.

Lord, yours is the pond, mine are the pebbles. Yours is the destination every ripple is longing to reach. Lord, let the ever-widening circle of the prayer pebbles I have tossed become a part of other ripples circling the pond and let our praise and petitions reach a place where perhaps...we will find the shore is made of all the prayer pebbles we have tossed and the pebbles are beautiful because they are called answers...It is a safe shore and the name of the place is peace.

Margaret Taylor Gilmore
September 4, 2003

Counting Candles

Edna Saint Vincent Millay wrote: "My candle burns at both ends, it may not last the night, but Oh, my foes and Oh, my friends, it gives a lovely light." I've been remembering those words and have thought how well they express the way I feel about my candle, now that I am nearing the end of my years.

I have wondered if perhaps Edna may have been musing one morning, thinking another birthday was near, and growing older was not in the future, but had already happened.

Perhaps she wrote those lines with just a bit of youthful rebellion to be read by younger people who would be surprised to be reminded her candle was not yet all used up.

Whatever inspired her to put those words on paper, we can bask in the glow of the flame of her candle. Her words are filled with thankfulness, even joy. She seems to say, "Listen everybody, you who love me and you who don't, I have had a wonderful life, and my mind is filled with rich memories. I am grateful to have lived long enough to have experienced breath-taking heights of gladness and unfathomable depths of sadness. I am thankful because most of my life has been an adventure in finding my way as I experienced the events and emotions that made my memory candle rich with scented wax."

I believe Edna wrote that statement at a time when she was feeling glad she had lived so long and because her mind was rich with memories of years and of moments that still glowed softly in the diminishing light of her days.

Birthdays come and years pass, and candles flame briefly on cakes, but their numbers are not always reflective of the lovely light that glows within a forever youthful heart.

Margaret Taylor Gilmore
July 12, 2005

Mysteries

The endless tide. Eternity. The Alpha and the Omega. The great I AM. Birth. Beginning. Ending. Death. Forever. Who, what, when. The perfect circle.

How much of the meaning of these terms are possible for us to actually intellectually fully comprehend? All of them hold hints of mystery...We somehow sense that if, within the definition of any of them, we could really grasp their total meaning, there would be real possibilities for gaining fulfillment that would make us wiser, more moral, more certain of who we are, and why we are such mysteriously motivated mortals.

What IS truth? What is life? What is holy? What is the holy? Is there anyone capable of understanding the meaning of a "holy mystery?"

It seems logical to me that if we are born of the spirit, and if the spirit dwells within us and if we continue to dwell within the spirit, then alive or in death we are already a part of eternity. Because from birth, emerging from the depths of God's purposes, we are created to be at home in the endless, ever-moving tide that is the sea of eternity. Sometimes, for awhile, we are almost satisfied and content, sometimes we are not. "Life is a mystery," we quote to each other.

While we live visibly as created human beings, we are known, named and take our place among the living. When we die, we become invisible to the world's eyes, but are the same spirit that was our spirit when we were visible. Now we are within the waves of eternity's tides along with others who joined the company of the ages before us. Who we were, we will always be. God's purposes and plans are always known to Him. That is the answer to most of our questions, if we have ever asked. Within God's eternal everlastingness here or there, He is forever watching over us, always ready, always willing to help us find our way from earth to heaven. There we will discover that love is the personification of the great I AM...and are within an endless perfect circle of love that includes all whom we have ever loved and perhaps had thought we had lost for awhile.

Margaret Taylor Gilmore
May 16, 2002

Seasons of Life

Today is the morning of the first day of autumn. My clock has struck eight times, sunlight is pale, and I am pensive. Those facts add to a questionable total, and I am writing here to find an answer, perhaps the answer to what my mind is needing to know. I am aware each morning that each day is different. The birds know too, and as I listen to them at dawn, I notice they speak in short, staccato stanzas, not in lengthy love songs of springtime. They know the season is autumn...

I have been contemplating what Paul Tournier wrote in his book, *The Seasons of Life*. The fourth chapter is *Winter*, life's final season. Tournier was sixty when he wrote that book, so his chapters describing the inevitable advancing years are from his personal experience.

That his book, that I read at least forty years ago, has unexpectedly returned to my hands, would seem randomly incidental, except for its timeliness. This is the autumn season of this present year and perhaps could be considered significant, especially now in America's ongoing seasons of its national life history.

In addition to the reassurance I have found in re-reading Tournier's book, I have shared copies of chapter four, *Winter*, with several friends. Each of them expressed real appreciation for the clear interpretation his words hold.

Tournier makes a comprehensive analysis of what he believes is the most valuable possession a person growing older owns, and what we leave when time has overtaken our earthly life. He says it is the total of the WHO we ARE that has lasted...It is the total of the who we tried to be, to do, to become, and the who we actually were in our springtime, summer, autumn and winter years.

Autumns almost always come sooner than expected. It seems as if overnight something has changed. In the autumn season of life we dwell on thoughts of the ways we expressed the who we were in springtime and in summer. Then, when winter will no longer be denied, memories take the pilgrim back to years of seasons that were springtimes, summertimes and the who we were in the afterglow of our autumn time. Then autumn is the season when the warmth of seasons past returns in remembering, it eases the chill in a winter-bound heart.

What remains of us that lasts forever are the moments that mattered when we were meeting the ordinary challenges of each day and made decisions that made someone's day better, brighter, and we thanked God for the occasions of opportunity.

Tournier, born in Switzerland, wrote in French. *Seasons of Life* was translated into English by John Gilmour.

Margaret Taylor Gilmore
September 21, 2005

Random Thoughts

"Through many dangers, toils and snares, I have already come...I have no less days to sing thy praise than when I first begun..."

What do I do now, God? Have I come this far, on faith most of the time, to arrive again in an unexpected climate of questioning and lack of direction in the time of life when I thought that by now almost everything would have been more or less firmly nailed down...But today I am still wondering, still somehow half expecting to find the map of my future clearly defined...

I have felt the call, and have followed my heart. I can look back and know that there WAS a map, and I followed it, but did it by Braille, as it were. God has not failed me in the past, why can I not be content to trust now in what I cannot see...after all the reassurances I have experienced?

"And Abraham went out, on faith to a strange country..."

Now...am I destined to go on traveling into yet another strange country? Or is it that I am to simply go back to being what I have been at this place for all this time, and cast my nets in the same waters? Is it that I should look for newness in the old places, and for catches beyond those I see coming into my nets?

"Cast your nets, He said, "on the other side of the boat...And lo, there were more fish than they could bring up in their nets..."

My good friend-pastor-preacher, Ed Coleman, says confidently, in his quiet Gibraltar way, that God will not abandon us, but that God will refresh, restore and fill our nets if we go out on faith and cast our trust into the ocean of His love...

By now I should not need to be reminded that God's grace is sufficient to provide everything necessary to my life. And I should not have to be told, over and over, that God doesn't play games with his children, no matter how many or how few years they are...And that life maps are not provided because if all things were known to us we would have no need to trust, or practice faith...the spiritual exercises that make us more fitted creatures for God's presence.

So...is the far, strange country a place where I should move my physical body...or is it a new, far reach into faith where I have not as yet gone to cast my nets to glean, perhaps a kind of "fish" that I had not yet known existed for me?

My friend offered us compasses and communion. He too is a pilgrim...on his own journey through his personal wildernesses and anxiously at times, I am sure he watches the waves for instructions as to which side of his boat to put down his nets...What do we do now, God? We will continue to come together in our mutual acknowledgement of needs, questions, uncertainties, and we will listen and respond, and taste the bread and wine together at the altar, and go out blessed, taking our nets and our joy at being a part of these holy mysteries. No maps...better than that...Sunday mornings I find a "fellowship of followers."

Margaret T. Gilmore
February 8, 1983

Seasons and Solstices

The Summer Solstice has passed. As I sat, watching dawn softly approaching, I was thinking that just a few hours ago, I had observed how gently darkness had touched the scene before me, and lately how many mornings had been silent of the voices of all those song birds that had so joyfully welcomed every dawn since Easter morning...Obviously, I thought, some voice within them has told them something is about to change.

To me there is something magical about those quiet moments when night's darkness is overcome by a gentle light, and then I am awed to witness at evening time, when the darkness returns to once again overtake the light. But now and then, a subtle change begins. I remember it was my grandfather who explained for me the meaning of the word, solstice, and how it changes the coming and going moments between our dawns and sunsets. Lately, this solstice season has set me to comparing how like our life is lived like the advent of a Summer Solstice, preparing for the Winter Solstice. There are lessons to be learned when we pause to observe the patterns that predict the rhythms of the seasons.

In the part of the world where I live, the late days of June bring the end of the birthing season of many garden flowers, and the beginning of warm days that hint of scorching sunlight that will bear down in days ahead. But today, the lovely delicacy of spring lingers, and frequent soft showers and brief morning mists have made us eager to meet summer, whatever temperatures it may bring.

And on mornings like this...my heart beats with a rhythm of thankful joy that I live in a place as lovely as this. Then I think about summer with its irrepressible confidence that it can win over any shadowy sky. But I remember the sweet sadness of autumn when darkness begins to cool some of those hours of blazing suns. And it is autumn that can make us romantic and mystify our minds as we marvel at the rise of those huge, yellow moons. And in September we begin to see and feel something new is about to happen and then, almost overnight, October arrives and releases floods of scarlet and gold leaves to fall over every hill and valley.

Then November's chilling winds blow over us and we are not surprised when winter seems to triumph for awhile, and we settle back to wait. We seldom contemplate that since the end of August, in a place somewhere, earth's heart is steadily beating and in her secret way she is moving silently beneath us, watching seeds that are sleeping and roots that are resting from making leaves and trees that are drinking from rivers that are running effortlessly from an endless source.

Meanwhile nights have lengthened and we try to make the most of the short hours when the sun is clearly in sight. Sometime around mid-February someone asks, "When is Easter this year?" And then someone may mention we will soon turn our clocks ahead one hour. We adjust our lives to fit the changes on the clock.

Life is like that, season to season, one at a time, while our hearts beat a rhythm of one at a time, and we live one moment, one day, one year at a time. Sometimes we count the sunset moments when darkness begins to overshadow the lingering light and we wonder how and why...Sometimes we simply take life one day at a time and know that only God knows what time it is for each of us.

But this is a day the Lord has made, and I am glad to be in it...Because this morning I saw a day being born as it emerged from the eastern horizon. Whatever signal Someone sent to call the sunrise at dawn, I am content to believe I can always trust that it will always shine somewhere...This is a beautiful morning and I am thankful, and as I begin to say so, I communicate with that part of me that knows my name. It is my "inner voice" with whom I speak.

I have wondered about this "voice" and have asked myself to tell myself what to believe is the source of the "other part of me" that is constantly speaking in my thoughts.

I have found my answer in the scripture that says we are to worship the Lord with our body, MIND and spirit. I believe I can trust the Voice within when I have prayed that my thoughts be acceptable unto Him.

Because I believe every breath we take is God's life giving breath, bearing fresh supplies of strength to every drop of our blood that flows through our body, and as we breathe out, we exhale impurities that God's clean air has cleansed from our veins. And because I believe He is the part of me that worships Him in prayer, I believe it is the part of Him who lives in me and gives me glimpses of glory as I experience Him in the rhythms of the beating of my heart and in the seasons that I see in dawns and sunsets.

Remembering grandfather explaining the meaning of the solstices and today...something...has led me to think that the word might also apply to the rhythms of my life, of the ever cycling seasons that came and went during which I learned more and more about who and what I am.

This morning as I thought as I wrote...my memory swept across the span of years, and of my grandfather's presence that throughout my life has stayed at the back of my mind...This morning I thought perhaps it is because I sense Grandpa's presence so often as I meditate and pray...Often when people have asked me if, and how...I picture in my thoughts how God might look, I always say, "Like my grandfather." I remember him as a large man with lots of white hair and bushy white eyebrows. I was a little afraid of him and wanted never to cause him anger...even though I don't recall ever seeing him angry...but I always knew he loved me. I wanted to please him, and when I did foolish childlike sins, I've thought that somehow he knew...but chose not to punish me, but to let me suffer because I think I knew he knew somehow that I knew just how much it would disappoint him if he knew.

This morning I have been wondering...is it Grandpa, or is it the voice of the great God Almighty, to whom I pray believing that to Him no secrets are hid and all desires known? Or is it the part of me that is born of the Holy Spirit...that speaks in my thoughts during all those conversations...to keep me mindful that I am an authentic child of God?

My heart tells me to believe in the voice within, because it is the best of who I am in conversation with the one who knows my name, hears me when I pray and continues to reassure me saying, "In all thy ways acknowledge me and I will direct your path."

Today I believe more than ever that I can trust the voice within. And I think perhaps that is the same voice Grandpa heard and followed instinctively on which to act, to speak, and how to decide which path to take throughout the many years of the solstices and seasons of his life.

Margaret Taylor Gilmore

End Things, Beginning Things
Measuring Moments

I woke today thinking of "end things." The end of my years, for example. And after I read Ezekiel, Chapters 31 and 32, my thought was that the message for me today is to notice, in those long repetitious verses, how carefully Ezekiel describes the way every part of a great temple was being measured. I believe I am to take note that every moment of life can be measured as an important event. The mysterious concept of those temple measurements is too deep, too wide, too high for me to fully grasp. But I do believe the Lord God Almighty designs and measures every detail of every thing that is, was and will be, and I also know that the one who measures us...is measureless.

And so I am thinking of taking a measurement of the years of my life. And of the ways and the means by which I can perhaps contemplate the size of the place reserved for me in heaven. What would be the measure of the house I have built in heaven? How thoughtfully, how carefully have I made choices, how faithful have I been to follow what I have learned about the presence of God in my life?

First, my thoughts turned to memories of my beginning times and of my first memory of being aware I was a person being present in a moment, of seeing myself separate, apart, yet connected in relationship with other persons. I woke, lying in bed beside my mother, and my father was on her other side. Now, as I remember how I felt, it was as if I had become awake for the first time. I must have been a very young child when that happened, but I have thought of that moment countless times.

My next clearest memory of being...present...was on a moonlight evening when I was being carried on my father's shoulders, on our way to my grandparent's home. My father was singing, "There's a long, long trail a-winding, into the land of my dreams..." That is my first memory of hearing a song and perhaps I remember that night because it was music made of moonlight and melody and I was sharing my father's memories of remembered longings. He had returned from the first Big War. Love and longing can compose songs in the heart.

I remember being told my mother wanted to see me, and they took me into where she was lying. I was uncomfortable, and did not want to linger there. Now I wonder why. But now I know she was about to die, and she knew it. At her funeral Uncle Frank held me up so I could look into her coffin, but I did not want to look.

Then there is the memory of being five years old, riding in a Model T Ford, on our way, Grandpa and Grandma Taylor and daddy and me...to live in Colorado. I remember arriving at the house where we lived for all my "growing up years," and where both my grandparents later died.

My memory is rich with memories of those next years. And one in particular is the night I saw a lady, dressed in a long white garment, standing in the light of a doorway between the bedroom and our "front room." She was moving slowly, lifting her arms to brush her long hair aside from her face. Thinking it was grandmother I spoke to ask for a drink, but Grandma's voice answered from across the room. My little bed was in a corner across the room from the big bed where my grandparents slept. I was startled and covered my head with the sheet. What I saw had been so clearly a person, of that I am still certain, and still wondering. I am no longer afraid of what I saw, but I have wondered many times why I did not tell anyone about that incident until I was grown.

I believe there is a secret place inside every one of us, a space known only to the exact person we are, and to that one who speaks within us. I believe from the moment we become aware of being one among others like us, that inner voice can make us aware of things that are beyond our power to comprehend. The voice makes us sensitive to beauty, to danger, to opportunity, to mystery and to things that are truly pure...

Through childhood I lived a quiet, private life, and for a while there were no neighbors with children to play with except at school, but I have no memory of ever being lonely. I loved all our animals, and I recall that I tearfully objected the day someone came to cut down an old tree in our yard. Grandpa said, "Oh well, let it stand."

I remember my first day at school. I wore a yellow dress with a large bow tied at the back. My teacher's name was Miss Bowlby. That day when I was returning from school, I have a distinctly vivid memory of Grandpa, sitting on the porch, welcoming me, saying, "Well, here comes our little scholar." I didn't know then what being a scholar meant, but it sounded like something Grandpa liked, and forever thereafter, I have always wanted to be a scholar.

I doubt it was because I was a scholar in the second grade when I was called out of class one day to be told I had been chosen to have a "lead part" in a school play that would be at Christmas in the "big auditorium." Now I know it wasn't a great part, because most of it was about things that took place while I pretended to be asleep. But I've wondered why I was chosen from among several others for what seemed to be an important part of the program. And now I wonder why it is one of the memories that created in me a feeling of being one among many. Perhaps it was my first experience in being "called out" from the crowd.

Mrs. Alice Houston was my fifth grade teacher. I remember the day I read aloud a paper she had assigned the class to write. We were to describe something we had seen, heard or felt that had seemed interesting. I wrote about the scent of steam rising from damp wood chips warmed by early morning sunlight. Her words set me on the path of my life's professional and personal achievements. Some sixty years later I learned where she was living and was able to write to thank her. Receiving her response letter to me is a shining moment among my memories.

World War II was rumbling throughout the world when I was graduating from high school. I remember that night wearing a long white dress, holding a red rose. I was seated beside a boy who was one of the first of our class to be killed at the beginning of World War II. I remember being suddenly made aware that all of us were at a point in our lives that I now call one of our "end time things." I still feel sad, remembering that night, because I never again saw most of those classmates with whom I had shared twelve years. That night was the beginning of the end of my "age of innocence."

The years of my early maturity were probably no different from the experiences of most young adults of my generation. But the world was churning with change and remembering those years, now it seems to me I was swept along by tides over which I had little control. Today, nearing the end of more years than I had ever expected to live, I take stock of how far I have come, and today am attempting to put into a few words, like chapter titles, how I look back on who I was then, am today, and perhaps will always be...

I have known, almost from the beginning that it was at the birth of my son that I first became aware I was to fulfill a specific role in the awesome ongoing-ness of my generation. Seeing his face for the first time, I thought he resembled my grandfather. And I knew without knowing why I knew, that he was God's child, and would live always aware somehow that what he knew about his Father God was true.

It was at that time I became more aware of being an individual with a role to play on a stage as large as my life would last. Looking back today, it was as if I had met the stranger who was walking with me on the Road to Emmaus...

And it was then that I began to depend on prayer. God became a secure presence, and I was no longer haunted by the words spoken to me by a neighbor who had said, "You should be ashamed. Your poor mother in heaven is grieving because you have not walked down the aisle during the revivals to be saved." Those yearly spring and fall tent revivals scared me, because when I watched people who were being saved do strange things. They often walked up and down the rows, sometimes trying to tug people to walk with them to the altar. Sometimes they raised their arms high and shouted loud things, or made outcries of words I could not understand. Most of them wept at times, and none of that kind of thing made me want to do the same. I dreaded revivals.

I truly believe it was at the birth of my son that I was "saved." I had never been around a newborn, let alone a toddler, but I knew I knew how to take care of this child, and something told me that now I was a completed person. My impression grew that we were together in special bond, held secure in God's presence. I remember praying he would not have to die in a war.

My memory of the day snow fell for the first time after Tad was born is bathed in a sort of haze of a moment I have learned to call "bliss." I held him, wrapped in a blue blanket and we were out where the large, fast falling snowflakes could fall on us. I said, "It's snow, Tad, it's snow, isn't snow wonderful?" Flakes fell on his eyelashes and I loved him and the snowflakes in a moment that became unforgettable.

I am thinking of my birth, my beginning and of the who and what I am today, and how I have found my way thus far. This morning I am thinking everything I have done, decided, been able to accomplish, all the inspiration and all the dangers, all the times I have experienced. I am certain an inner voice of a powerful presence has led, guided, protected and provided what I needed for my every moment. I was unaware then I was building my life. Or more exactly...that my life was being built around me.

But through the years I have felt a growing awareness of how powerful were the influences that seemed to be taking charge of my moments and my days. By mid-life I was becoming more distinctly aware that to put my trust in Jesus for guidance, was the only way I could find my way through the maze of the roles I had been chosen to play. Because by then I had begun to realize how profoundly important was my personal influence on many people's lives. That thought made me both humble and thankful. It made me think perhaps I was beginning to become even more like Grandpa Taylor.

Today, contemplating end things, I am remembering beginning things and wondering about the now things in my life that seem to matter now...I am wondering why I think some things I am doing now are important to be remembered after I am gone.

Then I remember birth, life and death happens to everyone, and am remembering how clearly I have been led and how sincerely I have trusted the One who made me, and enabled me to play this fascinating role on the stage of my life. God's presence has been my guide, protector, and the one who has healed me of my heart's wounds and strengthened my body's parts. He has inspired me, and answered when I prayed for help, and when I tell Him thank you, He blessed me even more. My spiritual "Braille" prayers have revealed God's grace and kept me safe...guided, provided for, and inspired. I have depended on prayer, because life has shown me I have no other way to "feel my way' through life's swift moving tides. I call it "spiritual Braille."

But there have been times I have asked, "Is this from YOU, God? Are you really still in charge of my journey? This doesn't seem to be in accord with what I thought you would send into my life." But every problem, every question has been the doorway to a blessing in disguise.

There have been moments when I have stood still, feeling totally vulnerable because so much was being required and expected of me, and I have called out to Him a prayer...of desperation, "Right now, Lord, as of this moment it's just me and You. Please take control. If I get through this safely, it will be because you enabled me to handle things...Lead on, O King Eternal." And He always has.

I was past mid-life when I experienced a matchless moment at the altar of St. Michael's Episcopal Church. Ever since that day, kneeling to receive communion, and I taste the wafer and feel the slight sting of the wine on my lips, I feel the presence of the one whose body and blood are symbolically in the moment. And I am renewed, reassured, restored and ready to meet whatever lies in the path of my days.

I am wondering why I am wondering why I am still living after so many years. This morning I am asking..."Could it be, Holy Father God, that you have even more for me to learn? Am I still a becoming scholar, and is construction still ongoing on my heavenly home? Is there more you have for me to do, to say, to write, to BE?" Am I being measured for further construction?

I am remembering shining moments this special morning...and I sense the Holy Spirit's encouragement as I pray. I am reminded of moments when I have glimpsed angelic beings standing near when I was most vulnerable. So many times I have felt a nearness of the presence of a powerful being and been reassured. I have asked God for help when I meet people who needed to be noticed and I did not know what to say. But you spoke and I spoke and the moment was good.

There have been times when I have been so overwhelmed with thankful joy I could find no ways nor words to express the emotion that was overflowing in the depth of my soul...But I knew you knew.

Now, nearing my end time...What I have written is like an outline of what I could write that would be the tales I'd tell of the countless, amazing stories about the people who have been part of my life and of the shining moments among the "ordinary days" we shared. Some people have given me shining moments to remember forever just because I stopped one day to listen while they told me the story of their life.

There are times when I celebrate "secret anniversaries," remembering sacred moments shared with individuals I knew for certain loved me as much as I loved them. Individuals, who in their own personally unique ways gave me, out of their own heart's storehouse, the kind of divine love God uses to bless His children in mysterious and miraculous ways only He can arrange...

Afterthoughts

And as I contemplate "end things" and search for exact "spiritual" words to write that might measure the depth that may be in the meanings of my memories, I find the word love, seems now to have revealed an expanded definition. Perhaps love is like a blueprint of our heavenly home, each person's map individually drawn, and the house constructed, day by day, each moment measured by what we say and do. And perhaps those shining moments are part of the material that helps bind the house securely together as it is being built. But who can measure love?

Perhaps, when completed, our heavenly home will have rooms where we can display our spiritual treasures, some of which are collections of those shining moment memories. And perhaps it will be possible, and we will joyfully renew remembrances of those shining moments we shared before we moved into our homes in heaven.

Margaret Taylor Gilmore
June 4, 2005

What is Written is Written

"The moving finger writes, and having writ moves on. Nor can your tears, your piety nor wit remove a line of it." So wrote Gibran many years ago.

What I have written I have written, and all of it is from the welling up of the essences of my emotions as I experienced life. My fingers have written of my awe, my longings, and my loves, and of the sweetnesses and the sadnesses of having lived a full life. I have tried to put into words the impossible-to-describe rich colors of the emotions of my thankful, needful, fearful, prayerful, ever-searching spirit.

So I will not weep for dreams deferred, nor for forgiveness for praying for selfish gifts that I have uttered in moments of unexpected temptation.   I will give thanks for God's forgetting and forgiving when I forgot Him for a while. Of this I will write again, or sing again someday.

For what was written is written and within those lines there is the fragrance of the essences of days and nights of a life that God blessed with love abundant enough to share.

Margaret Taylor Gilmore
December 1, 2001

Printed in the United States
53406LVS00001B/1-102

9 780965 362450